CROSSDRESSING
WITH
DIGNITY

CROSSDRESSING WITH DIGNITY

The Case For Transcending Gender Lines

Peggy J. Rudd, Ed.D

PM Publishers
Katy, Texas

Published 1999 by PM Publishers

Crossdressing With Dignity: The Case For Transcending Gender Lines. Revised edition. Copyright ©1999 by Peggy Rudd, Ed.D. All rights reserved. Four printings from 1990 to 1999. No part of this book may be used or reproduced in any manner without written permission except in the case of brief quotations embodied in critical articles and reviews. For information contact PM Publishers, Inc., P.O. Box 5304, Katy, TX 77491-5304. Fax: 281-347-8747. Email: pmpub@pmpub.com, http://www.pmpub.com.

Publisher's Cataloging-in-Publication
(Provided by Quality Books, Inc.)

Rudd, Peggy J.
    Crossdressing with dignity: the case for transcending
    gender lines / Peggy J. Rudd. -- rev. ed.
    p. cm.
    Includes bibliographical references and index.
    Preassigned LCCN: 98-068036
    ISBN: 0-9626762-6-8

    I. Transvestism   I. Title

HQ77.R83 1999   306.77
                    QBI98-1385

Printed in the United States of America

ACKNOWLEDGMENTS

I am deeply grateful to each crossdresser who participated in the survey which served as the basis for this book. The research would not have been completed without your input. It would be wonderful to personally thank each individual who returned the questionnaire. Please know how valuable your participation was to this study, and how much you have contributed to the existing body of knowledge related to crossdressing.

I would like to thank Richard Docter, Ph.D, Jane Ellen Fairfax, M.D., Kathy Cloud and Frances Pasek for editorial assistance, friendship and encouragement. Each person spent many hours reading and editing the manuscript. Their wisdom strengthened the book throughout, even as their leadership strengthens the case for crossdressing with dignity.

Two special transgendered attorney friends, Catherine and Phyllis, were especially helpful in providing advice on the "guilt" chapter.

Last, but not least, I would like to thank my husband, Mel/Melanie, who not only edited, but also provided domestic services around the house as I pushed to meet deadlines. While in many ways the book is my gift to him/her, it has also been a personal sacrifice by him/her. Thank you Melanie, THE LOVE OF MY LIFE!

BOOKS PUBLISHED BY PM PUBLISHERS.

WHO'S REALLY FROM VENUS? The Tale of Two Genders by Peggy J. Rudd, Ed.D. The author provides valuable suggestions on how to live life to the fullest through the integration of masculinity and femininity. ISBN 0-962676241. 5 1/2" x 8 1/2". 176 pages. Perfect bound paperback. 36 photos of transgendered individuals and significant people in their lives. $15.95 retail price.

CROSSDRESSERS: And Those Who Share Their Lives by Peggy J. Rudd, Ed.D. 51 photos and numerous true stories depict the transformation of men from the masculine to the feminine persona. Dr. Rudd carefully details strategies for coping, both for the crossdresser and those who share their lives. This book was featured on the Leeza Show on NBC. ISBN 0-9626762337. 5 1/2" x 8 1/2. 113 pages. Perfect bound paperback. $14.95 retail price.

CROSSDRESSING WITH DIGNITY: The Case for Transcending Gender Lines by Peggy J. Rudd, Ed.D. Is society ready for men who openly express femininity? Can men transcend gender lines and maintain their sense of self-worth and dignity? These are questions asked to over 800 crossdressers in a survey used as the basis of this book. ISBN 0-962676268. 5 ½ x 8 1/2". 178 pages. Perfect bound paperback. $14.95 retail price

MY HUSBAND WEARS MY CLOTHES: Crossdressing from the Perspective of a Wife by Peggy J. Rudd, Ed.D. The first book on the unique topic of crossdressing written from the perspective of a wife. *"Clothes don't make the man",* has a new meaning. Dr, Rudd addresses many of the questions asked by the spouses, families and friends of men who crossdress. ISBN 0-96267625X. 5 1/2" x 8 1/2". 160 pages. Perfect bound paperback. $14.95 retail price.

LOVE CALENDAR: The Secrets of Love by Peggy J. Rudd Thorne, Ed.D. Dr. Thorne combines quotations with common sense applications. In this compassionate book, she encourages readers to spend five minutes daily in the *"Love Exercise."* **LOVE CALENDAR** is recommended for any couple seeking a happy, lasting relationship and those persons who are searching for love. ISBN 0-962676225. 5 1/2 x 8 1/2. 160 pages. Perfect bound paperback. $4.95 special price.

PREFACE

The Scottish male wears a kilt, but is society ready for men who openly express femininity? This is the question asked in a survey used as the basis for this book. Can a man transcend gender lines and maintain his own sense of self-worth and dignity?

From an early age boys are taught to follow the stereotypes of maleness. When the inner desire to express femininity exerts a greater force than the desire to live up to the appropriate image for masculinity, conflict may develop.

In his book, TRANSVESTITES AND TRANSSEXUALS: Toward A Theory Of Cross-Gender Behavior, Dr. Richard Docter describes the dilemma:

"When a heterosexual male presents himself to others with the appearance of a woman, and strives to imitate a woman, there is a confusing paradox. On the one hand, we have a more or less conventional male, often married, who seems to function satisfactorily in his various male roles. But on the other hand, he lives a secret second life dominated by fantasies of being a temporary, periodic woman, and he derives extraordinary exhilaration and delight in this. Despite the social disapproval which would almost surely accompany the public disclosure of his transvestism, he devotes much of his fantasy life and some of his time to periodic crossdressing."

As the wife of a crossdresser, my goal has been to write a provocative book addressing the emotions that surface when men transcend gender lines. I believe the book will help crossdressers overcome the emotions of guilt, fear, denial, hostility, and loneliness. As crossdressers move forward to inner peace and a sense of personal dignity, they will realize richer and more complete lives.

Since this book represents the collective input from more than 800 crossdressers, a wide spectrum of ideas, theories and philosophies is presented. It would be impossible for any reader to accept such a diversity of opinions at face value.

This book is dedicated to the butterfly who has inspired us to move beyond the gray cocoons of our lives and into a more beautiful existence.

CONTENTS

Chapter Nine:

SELF-ACCEPTANCE, FIND IT
WITHIN OR FIND IT NOT

Chapter Ten:

YOU ARE NEVER ALONE

CHAPTER ONE

INTRODUCTION

Don Juan: Your weak side, my diabolic friend, is that you have always been a gull: you take a man at his own valuation. Nothing would flatter him more than your opinion of him. He loves to think of himself as bold and bad. He is neither one nor the other. George Bernard Shaw, MAN AND SUPERMAN

A number of years ago I discovered the truth in the George Bernard Shaw quote. My husband was neither bold nor bad, but other words had been used to describe him. He was sometimes called a crossdresser, a man who enjoys wearing women's clothing. The word, femmophile was used to describe his love for femininity. At other times he was simply called a transvestite. For me, "bold and bad" carried less social stigma than any of these terms.

My frustrations led to a quest for truth and understanding, and ultimately to my first book, MY HUSBAND WEARS MY CLOTHES. The book described our experiences of overcoming the social stigmas, and examined the issues often raised by spouses, family members and friends of crossdressers. Acceptance was described as a legitimate goal that can be rewarding for those who love crossdressers.

CROSSDRESSING WITH DIGNITY: The Case For Transcending Gender Lines paves the path for crossdressers as they enter a hostile world. Society places the crossdresser in a defensive position, but I believe the time has come for us to move ahead with our lives. It is possible to be a crossdresser and maintain a personal sense of dignity. This book may help in the developmental process so that the individual will accept who they are. The end result should be a personal growth which leads to self-fulfillment.

THE MEANING OF DIGNITY

A person can transcend gender lines and still be a dignified person. THE WORLD BOOK DICTIONARY gives the definition of dignity used in this chapter. It defines dignity as, "a proud and self-respecting character or manner." While it is important to be perceived by others as a person with dignity, the theme of this book will relate to the quality of life within the individual. It is possible to be a crossdresser and feel proud of whom you are. It is possible for a person's thoughts and actions to be dignified even if the individual is perceived by society as, "different." Connie, a cross-dresser, believes she can experience dignity when an effort is made to understand others:

> *"We should try to understand the fears of society, since fear causes society to ridicule or dislike us. There will be less fear when each crossdresser does these things:*
>
> *1. Dress and act like a lady.*
>
> *2. Refrain from arguments.*
>
> *3. Resist the temptation to force yourself upon others.*
>
> *4. Show yourself to be a caring individual.*
>
> *5. Like yourself and carry yourself in high esteem.*
>
> *6. Tell those closest to you how much you love them. "*

THE BASIS FOR THE BOOK

Early in the process of writing CROSSDRESSING WITH DIGNITY, I searched for references from the massive library at the University of Texas in Austin, Texas. I found some noteworthy research from social scientists who committed large amounts of their time and talent to understanding transvestism. While much of what I found was relevant, I instinctively knew my most valid point of reference would be from the crossdressing community itself. A questionnaire was included in the January 1990, issues of the FEMME MIRROR, the publication of Tri-Ess, a national organization of crossdressers and their partners. The questionnaire was sent to more than 1000 crossdressers. It was also provided to participants of the Compuserve Computer Bulletin Board Service (BBS), Tri-Ess BBS, Carolyn's Closet BBS and the Jersey Shore Computer BBS. Crossdressing organizations nationwide and in Canada distributed the questionnaire to their membership. (A copy of the questionnaire is included in Appendix A).

More than 800 crossdressers returned completed question-naires. The responses served as the dominate basis for this book. Because the population used in this research was so extensive, the validity seems evident. The responses came back in many forms. Some were written on perfumed paper. Others were on professional letter heads or computer printouts. Some answers were given as one word responses, while other respondents sent documents of up to a hundred pages.

The questionnaires were received from small towns and large cities. Many crossdressers enclosed lovely photographs and personal letters. There were poems, funny stories, and sad accounts of lives tarnished by anxiety and frustration. The responses came from the hearts of people who desired to be considered dignified and worthy. The research file represents the pulse of the crossdressing population.

Respondents described the stigmas imposed by society as well as the obstacles that are self-imposed. In the process of completing the questionnaire, each person looked into the heart for truth about fears, feelings of guilt and loneliness. In moving, personal stories they told about their human relationships and how crossdressing had affected their lives. Some described joys; others described frustration and heartache. They told of their quest for self-worth, dignity, understanding and acceptance.

It became apparent that answering the questionnaire provided an introspection. Mira La Cous had this experience:

"Please find enclosed my responses to your question-naire I found on Carolyn's Closet BBS in St. Paul, Minnesota; I hope you don't mind me calling you, Peggy, but in sharing this much of my personal self I needed to get a little closer to you.

Providing answers to your questions, I was able to more fully understand myself, and what I must do to move in the direction of self-acceptance. I felt I had accepted my crossdressing, but I had not. Thank you for taking time to make crossdressing known to the public in a good light, and aiding crossdressers in understanding what and who they are. "

WHO NEEDS THIS BOOK?

Anyone who is interested in gender related issues should read this book. It is certainly a "must" for crossdressers and others who share their lives. I believe the value of the book will extend far beyond this limited population. If you want to know how social experiences have shaped your attitudes about gender, this book is important. Persons who may be helped include:

1. Helping professionals who specialize in gender issues.

2. Educators who teach courses in sociology, psychology, anthropology, cultural issues or human sexuality.

3. People in the general public who have an interest in broadening their awareness about human nature.

4. Statisticians who compile diagnostic data related to mental disorders. (DSM-IV - Revised) Professionals now believe crossdressing is a deviation from the norm, but they no longer equate crossdressing with mental illness.

5. Theologians who may counsel crossdressers or their families.

6. Talk show hosts desiring a broader and more honest perception of crossdressing.

7. "Tabloid Tycoons" who may write a human interest story about people who express two genders.

WHAT IS THE PURPOSE OF THIS BOOK?

CROSSDRESSING WITH DIGNITY: The Case for Transcending Gender Lines was written to help people deal with crossdressing in a constructive manner. Crossdressing is not harmful, but a fear of it and a lack of understanding can breed prejudice and contempt. This book will show that for some people crossdressing is a basic human need, highly charged with many emotions.

One dominant emotion presented is fear, an obstacle that must be overcome if crossdressers are to learn to accept themselves. Moving beyond   the fear of self is the first step. Next the crossdresser will deal with the fear of society and the fear of alienation and rejection. Guilt is the second major emotion addressed. Crossdressers are encouraged to take responsibility for their actions, trace the origins of the guilt feelings and develop a pattern that will prohibit guilt imposed by others.

The book shows the process of moving away from negative emotions toward strong self-esteem and a feeling of self-worth. Respect is not something society owes the crossdressing community. Rather it begins within the heart of a person and is projected outward into the eyes of observers. "Taste is the feminine of genius," wrote Edward Fitzgerald in 1877. Perfecting feminine deportment and demeanor will be presented as the prerequisites of respect. Once perfected, the transgendered community will earn the sanction of society.

HOW DO YOU USE THIS BOOK?

Topics and sub-topics are carefully outlined in the Table of Contents. Each chapter is written as a separate entity that can stand alone. The chapters relate to the total theme of the book - the development of an inner feeling of self-dignity. A glossary is provided for readers who need clarity for the vocabulary that in some ways is unique to the crossdressing community. The Appendix includes research data obtained from the questionnaire. CROSSDRESSING WITH DIGNITY is intended to be a book that will motivate self-improvement, introspection. and awareness of gender issues.

Dignity is not created by what has happened to us,
but by our attitude about our destiny.

CHAPTER TWO

IN QUEST OF DIGNITY

The quest for dignity is like a mountain high,
Rare is the air and blue. It is a long hard climb,
With tremendous fatigue,
But oh! What a wonderful view.

THE SCOTT FORESMAN DICTIONARY defines DIGNITY as, "the degree of worth, honor and importance." During the past years I have made a quest for dignity at the side of Melanie, my crossdressing husband. While we have felt dignified in many aspects of our lives, incorporating these feelings into the context of crossdressing has been a greater challenge. It has been very much like a mountain climb with obstacles all along the way. For every step forward, there were two steps backwards. We saw an ocean of faces and many of them reflected contempt.

A WALK TROUGH JUDGMENT

As a new bride the possibility of rejection by family and friends was very frightening. For Melanie there was the tendency to look back with regret on all the years before we had met. Both of us knew the problems of the present could be overcome if we pooled our strengths. As we held hands and looked toward the future the need to bind up the wounds seemed evident. Yes, there were reasons to feel hurt. There had been an emotional challenge, but nursing wounds only made the situation seem worse.

In our quest for dignity, we were forced to look judgment squarely in the eye. Not only had society judged us, but we had judged ourselves. The knowledge that we were involved in something outside of "normal" caused some discomfort. It sometimes seemed like self-delusion to think we could fit into society's mold. Terre Anne, one of our friends from Carolyn's Closet BBS, agreed:

"Even if a crossdresser is passable, the probability of being 'read' and derisively treated is great. The only dignity a crossdresser has is self-dignity. When the artificial stigmas fostered through ignorance are removed, crossdressers will be treated as valuable members of society."

Because of our social conditioning, we had to learn to handle or dissipate guilt. The process involved sorting out the valid expectations of society from the invalid ones and tempering the sorting process with the gender issue. Donna Mobley added this comment, "If a crossdresser can reach a level of self-acceptance and self-respect, and stop feeling like there's something wrong, then a measure of dignity seems to follow as a matter of course. We can't let society determine our self-worth for us."

THE DILEMMA

The word "lemma" means "a proposition which we assume to be true." In a DILEMMA there are two propositions that are equally true. A DILEMMA, therefore, involves a choice between two distinct elements. This was one of the first things I learned about Melanie. She was in touch with two parts of her personality, the masculine and the feminine. But before Melanie understood how the two parts could be integrated, she felt the dilemma.

I felt totally confused, because Melanie had not told me about her crossdressing prior to marriage. My dilemma related to the fact that I still perceived "her" to be a "him." Because our relationship was the most important part of my life, many questions needed to be analyzed and resolved. "Am I responsible for the crossdressing? What have I done? How can I help?"

Melanie told me I was not at all responsible; the urge came from within. She further explained how the dressing had given her the feeling of actually "being" a woman. This explanation didn't come close to satisfying me. As a woman I had experienced the physiological aspects of womanhood firsthand, such as childbirth. I had also experienced the sociological roles of wife and mother. It was difficult for me to understand how dressing and wearing makeup could bring a person of the opposite sex into that level of empathy. What did seem obvious, however, was Melanie's ability to understand some aspects of feminine expression. There was definitely an appreciation of womanhood.

The definition of a dilemma, found in the WORLD BOOK DICTIONARY, stresses the unpleasant nature of decision making. A dilemma is literally an argument forcing a person to choose one of two equally unfavorable alternatives. For Melanie to choose to be totally masculine would be an unpleasant alternative, since this choice would suppress the finer feminine qualities such as compassion, tenderness and gentleness. Choosing to be Melanie all of the time would be equally unpleasant. On the personal side, I married a man and not a woman. Losing the masculine personality I fell in love with, would be most unpleasant. Herein lies the dilemma. While the walk through judgment caused us to look outward into the society that had scorned us, the real cause of concern was the dilemma of self-identity and the adjustments needed for new life scripts.

Rachel explained the balance of personality traits or a blend, and expressed her realization that crossdressing is a valuable part of her otherwise masculine personality:

"I try to not let either set of characteristics dominate the other. 'The sum of the parts is greater than the whole.' If integration can be achieved, the crossdresser is ready to challenge society's concept of crossdressing with dignity and pride, and it will be translated to society in a positive way. There is also the realization that nothing is perfect, and our femininity and society's perception of our femininity will never be exactly as we desire. With that realization comes an enjoyable pursuit of making social perception progressively clearer for generations to come. "

THE CLOTHING ISSUES

The clothing Melanie wore became an issue for a while. The first time I saw her she was dressed very much like a streetwalker.

In earlier discussions Melanie had explained crossdressing related to a love of womanhood. Thus, a whole new area of confusion emerged. If the "hooker" image was what she admired, then I was surely not her ideal woman.

The issue became compounded by Melanie's interest in magazines that feature the "hooker" image of femininity, such as PENTHOUSE and PLAYBOY. She explained how much enjoyment was felt while looking at beautiful women, but was careful to add that her love for me was separate and apart from the pleasure gleaned from the pictures. At this point I became even more confused. If I was the object of her love, why couldn't I be the role model for the dressing? I felt these magazines and the girls on the street were the real inspiration for Melanie.

I am a very confident person, but the presence of the magazines in our home made me feel insecure. Even after our discussion, and Melanie's awareness of my disgust, I continued to find magazines hidden in the car. This reinforced their importance. At one point I was even confused about who got pleasure from the pictures. If the "Mel" part of the personality was enjoying the pictures, I felt jealous, because I wanted to be his sex object. If the magazines were seen through Melanie's eyes, I felt hurt, because I did not appear to be the kind of woman she wanted to emulate.

Thus the type of clothing Melanie had chosen and the kind of magazines she seemed to enjoy, opened up a new element of pain. What I had wanted, if the dressing was to occur, was to be a role model for Melanie. My style is natural, friendly and carefree. Four inch pumps and a makeup overdose do not portray who I am or how I want to be perceived as a woman. This caused me to wonder if Melanie was really happy with me as I am. I wanted to contribute to Melanie's transformation, to help with makeup and shopping, but it was impossible to relate to her expression of femininity. I pondered, "What is Melanie seeking in her image of femininity? Does Melanie want to emulate my type of femininity or will she want to look like the pictures?"

In time I found answers and Melanie found maturity and growth. At our house the fetishistic phase has passed, and I'll be the first to say, "I am glad!" Today Melanie is a lady, both in deportment and in appearance. I guess we have come full circle, because I now look up to Melanie as my role model. Thus, one of the obstacles in our quest for dignity has been overcome. Today there are no strict gender lines in our relationship, as we both strive to be the best people possible.

I know fetishistic dressing is a phase most crossdressers need to experience as a part of the validation process. For some the fetishistic phase never ends, but when the dressing moves beyond the security of home and into the public arena, discretion is needed Otherwise the transgendered community will remain buried under the harsh winds of criticism and scrutiny. We will continue to be judged as less than dignified.

Other crossdressers have shared their growth processes. Annette walked the path of fetishistic dressing, but believes improved judgement is the by-product of maturity.

"Crude forms of complete dressing were my starting point, but I have moved to where I am now, attempting to create a complete and credible feminine appearance that is non-offensive and as acceptable as possible in a wide variety of situations. The steps involve becoming far more conscious of what looks good on me rather than what I like on skinny 16 year-old girls. Careful observation of what women of my general build and age wear, what looks good and what doesn't, has helped me perfect an appropriate image. "

THE DREAM OF ACCEPTANCE

During the months that followed we came to realize how social acceptance may be only a dream. Some of our relatives seemed to put me in the same category as the wife of an alcoholic, or a battered and abused wife. One relative said, "You really don't have to stay in a marriage like that, and be treated with such abuse!" Meanwhile, Melanie's children who loved their father too much to verbally denounce their father for crossdressing, began to hurl all their anger toward me."If you would stop placating Dad's behavior, this awful habit would go away. You are wrong to support crossdressing. You are an enabler of a mental disorder!"

I knew I did not ask to be married to a crossdresser, but I also knew the very support we had given each other eased much of the pain that had been inflicted by an unsympathetic and frequently angry social system. Sharing the problem with each other and growing beyond the pain, was one experience which contributed to our rare and beautiful relationship.

We learned to resist judging the people who were judging us. Unfortunately we both knew even our closest loved ones may never accept Melanie.

A SOCIAL NIGHTMARE

If the people who professed to love us, could not accept Melanie's crossdressing there seemed little chance of acceptance by society. One of the questions on the questionnaire dealt with the dream of social acceptance. Some respondents said in effect, "If this is a dream, it must be a nightmare," Others, such as Donna Baker, woke up from the bad dream and voiced a respect for social attitudes:

> *"Whatever the reasons for it, society is much less ready to accept a man in women's clothes than to accept a woman in the reverse situation. I do not find this unfair. I was unable to discontinue dressing, in spite of trying very hard to do so. This tells me that the appeal is very deep-seated, not easily overcome by willpower. Judging by the pervasiveness of the distaste society has for crossdressers, I can easily believe this distaste may be just as deep seated and fundamental as my own need to dress. My need may very well be that aversion turned inside out or upside down by some experience in my childhood. I can't change myself and doubt society can significantly change.*
>
> *I don't wish to pressure society to accept a bearded*

lumberjack in a dress at Sears. I will apply pressure to make sure the store distinguishes between a store's right to refuse a lumberjack service and criminal prosecution for crossdressing. The later is definitely a violation of my liberty. "

A PERSONAL COMMITMENT

It seems that society's standards are a melange that includes millions of individual standards. The standards tend to change over time, but they change very slowly. It behooves us to scrape away at the primeval homo erectus buried deep within us and become committed to changing the social image crossdressers present.

There are simple rules that will make life easier. Begin by shaving the beard before venturing out in public in a dress. Limit fetishistic dressing to situations that are "safe" meaning "in a supportive environment." Portray the best possible image in situations that may be threatening to the reputation of the total transgendered community. I realize this concept may not be a popular for some crossdressers, but please give it some thought. Perhaps it would help to distinguish between social and personal rights.

While society will continue to make judgements when crossdressers present a less-than-credible image, Jane Ellen sees two niches in which society has no right to encroach:

"The first one includes situations in which the crossdresser is predominantly in the company of those portions of society that willingly accept this aspect of her behavior. This would include her home, a friend's home, clubs and businesses that cater to crossdressers.

The second niche lies in the educational process. It is very important that society allow young people to learn about various forms of gender related problems. Colleges and universities are now offering courses related to crossdressing. Through these courses young crossdressers discover that they will likely continue the practice. Potential wives discover there is no cure. Professionals are learning methods of offering help. It seems the educational process is moving in the right direction. "

Since it is necessary to provide information about gender issues to the people who need it, we should be aware of society's reluctance to deal with these issues. We should also constructively work against the attempts by some members of society to prevent us from fulfilling our needs in private or semi-public situations. Crossdressers have no more right to demand general acceptance by all, or even most, of the individuals in society, than they do to demand we cease the practice. The right to swing your arms ends where the other person's nose begins.

Kay feels the answer rests with educating the public and maintaining a good public image:

"It is only through heightened public consciousness that the stigmas can be removed. Each crossdresser must feel responsible for the public image. The media has been less than kind. Recently a local television station reported on a lady who was running for mayor in Northern California. While many women run for mayor, the one thing that made this a news item related to her sex change operation. Thus, even a positive description of her public service was turned into a negative statement. "

THE LIFE SCRIPT

When Melanie and I understood the reluctance of society to accept us, we realized a need to look closely at our life script. Some questions needed to be answered. "Who were we? What did all of this mean?" We tried to sort out what crossdressing was actually saying about our sexuality as well as what it was saying about the totality of our lives together. This was a time for putting things into perspective.

The purging ritual had already been attempted with no positive effect. Melanie told me she had destroyed and repurchased whole wardrobes. I am thankful her problems were not compounded by an attitude on my part that said, "Quit, or I'll leave you!" An ultimatum was not even considered, because I saw pain and agony in her face. Perhaps I believed her the first time she told me that quitting was not possible. We both knew crossdressing was indelibly written upon our life script. There was a time when we searched for solutions alone. At that time it seemed less of a social issue and more of a personal one.

T.S. Elliot's, THE COCKTAIL PARTY, described our feeling of being surrounded by people who do not understand:

> *"No, it isn't that I want to be alone,*
> *But that everyone's alone - or so it seems to me.*
> *They make noises, and think they are talking to each other.*
> *They make faces and pretend they understand each other.*
> *And I'm sure they don't. "*

LIVE ONE DAY AT THE TIME

There seemed to be a legitimate reason to face each new day with expectancy. Living one day at the time involved a commitment to each other and to our relationship. We knew our love could help us overcome the obstacles, and we could move toward personal dignity. We also knew that if we failed, it would be because we had consumed too much strength with memories of rejection and the dread of what might occur in the future. Therefore, our energies were redirected toward improving our relationship and our individual lives.

The story is told about a traveler who stopped at the general store in a small town. He asked the old gentleman behind the counter what the town was noted for. The old gentleman scratched his head in puzzlement and said, "This is the starting place for anywhere in the world. From here you can go wherever you want to go." Melanie and I knew we were at a starting place, and we could determine our direction.

WHERE TO FROM HERE?

As we looked forward to the rest of our lives, there were several choices. We could look back to the pain of rejection and the uncertainty that surrounded it, but we chose to progress forward by accepting femininity as a vital and dynamic part of Melanie's identity. We quit fighting the feminine emotions which she cherished and began to enjoy what these feelings could do for our relationship. Melanie accepted her birthright, and collectively our focus shifted to hope and reality.

There is no way for anyone to predict how social acceptance will change, but Melanie and I are committed to living each day to the fullest and being the best we can be. The enemy is not society. The real enemy is within our psyche: the inability to move forward and the tendency to hold on to a negative past. I see the development of Melanie and our relationship to be very much like the butterfly. She hid herself beneath the dismal gray of the cocoon - dormant, lifeless and void of feelings. She came forth in a great display of beauty to grace the presence of all.

Janette believes it is good to take the "plunge" and share who you are with those closest to you. She adds these optimistic ideas:

"When I shared what I know about myself with my significant other, she was understanding and tolerant of my special needs. Sharing was like taking the weight of the world off my shoulders. A change in personality was the result of being up front about myself. I was a much happier person, and that affected everything I did. "

Oscar Hammerstein wrote the moving song, CLIMB EVERY MOUNTAIN. In my daily activities, when I have difficulty being motivated to move forward, I can hear the resonant voice of the nun in SOUND OF MUSIC who sang the song. Later the von Trapp family began their climb over the mountain. Determined to not dilute their convictions, the family fled Austria rather than serve the Nazi Party regime. When we remember the great oppressions in history, we realize our problems are diminutive by comparison. Although we live in a society that does not understand us, we sometimes do not understand ourselves. When you feel heavy hearted, meditate upon these beautiful and inspiring words:

> *"Climb every mountain, Search high and low,*
> *Follow every byway, Every path you know.*
> *Climb every mountain, Ford every stream,*
> *Follow every rainbow. 'Til you find your dream"*

Our dream must be dignity! This is the desire of our hearts. The climb may be long, but we will give our best effort.

He who ascends to mountain heights,
Shall find the loftiest peaks wrapped in clouds and snow.
He who surpasses or subdues mankind,
Must look down upon the hatred of the world below.
A poem by Lord Bryan

CHAPTER THREE

OVERCOMING OBSTACLES

Knew...if I only knew why! What I can't bear is the blindness - meaninglessness - the numb blow fallen in the stumbling night.   Archibald Macleish

Chapter Two described our desire for dignity, and some thoughts about the endless search for answers to the proverbial question,"why?"This chapter will include perceptions of the transgendered as they attempt to overcome obstacles including the quest for balance and integration, self-acceptance and social respect. As crossdressers move forward into the world there will be challenges in the areas of relationships and education. Status and high position are not qualities of life that society "owes" the crossdressing community. Dignity is a personal state that begins within and is projected outward to others. How can crossdressers move in the direction of self-fulfillment? This chapter will examine social and personal aspects of living a dignified life.

Tomye Kelley, M.A., a psychotherapist who works with gender conflicted people and their significant others, has summarized the challenge. Kelley encourages crossdressers to look for ways to accept this particular part of themselves as just that - a part, not the whole. Kelley sees the real struggle as related to an image which is frequently tarnished by media:

"The transgender community is seeking acceptance without judgment. We struggle to present ourselves to our loved ones in a positive manner. Often I see members of the community beginning to succeed in that effort, only to have the media sensationalize an article that tells one part of our story, thereby grabbing headlines at the expense of this population. If the public's knowledge and attitude are to be improved, the transgendered community must participate in telling about their lives to the media thus projecting dignity and earning respect. "

Jane Ellen Fairfax sees integration as one solution:

"Our cross-gender traits are a part of us and not the whole. We are more than our feminine or masculine clothing. The best adjusted crossdressers have learned to integrate their cross-gender traits into their personalities. In this way these traits become a part of the whole, and results in a more balanced personality and positive public image."

BALANCING THE MASCULINE AND THE FEMININE

Rachel believes balance is one key as the transgendered move toward public acceptance.

"Without an internal feeling of the value of crossdressing, the crossdresser has bought society's imaginary evaluation. She should set realistic, attainable goals so when they are attained she can say, 'I like myself,' rather than, 'I knew I couldn't do it.'

The crossdresser should realize most of the stigmas imposed by society are in the imagination, and then use the value of her femininity to validate her masculinity. This is accomplished by taking the better parts of the masculine and feminine sides to form a stronger composite blend.

Many crossdressers seem to have an accelerated drift toward total femininity as they emerge. Some move toward transsexuality at this time. Others tend to ignore the down side of femininity or the up side of masculinity. They are like a chemical reaction, which proceeds to a state of equilibrium and an improved public perception."

When the crossdresser realizes the femme side of the personality can enhance the masculine traits, he will realize an improved personality. Overcoming social programming while attempting to blend into this society is the big hurdle. Once this is achieved, much of the guilt and fear will go away. The resulting self-image will shine through and be transferred to the public.

SELF-ACCEPTANCE

Moving in the direction of self-acceptance involves taking a long, hard look at guilt in an effort to determine which feelings are justified and which ones are not. Guilt "with cause" must be dealt with. If we have willingly harmed others through a lack of consideration, or some other hurtful act, we must reach out to the persons with love to make it right. If, however, our guilt is related to some unrealistic social expectation, we need to look closely at the stereotypes and accept our human differences. There is no reason to harbor needless guilt for being born a unique and special human with a broad range of gender expressions. Our unique qualities may be a cause for celebration and the path toward self-acceptance. Walk the path with confidence, and at the end of the way there will be an abundance of inner peace.

Self-acceptance comes easier for people who strive to do their best. This was one of the first lessons my parents taught me. Report cards, for example, were acceptable only if Mom and Dad believed I had put forth strong effort. I learned very early that accepting myself was tied to doing the best possible job. Commitment to the task and focus are driving forces in my life.

As crossdressers tell me stories of social or personal problems, I have often asked, "Have you done your best?" When we have tried to make things right, there is no need for self-rebuke, even in the face of social failure. When this lesson becomes a part of the force which propels us into the world, we will know that we have found the key. At that time we can collectively rise above a world which is full of ignorance, prejudice and half-truths. Each person must project the best possible image. The solution to social barriers can be found in our hearts. "It is OK to be a woman though male," to quote the very famous Virginia Prince.

Glenda Rene Jones feels that it is important to play the hand God dealt us to the best of our ability. The most powerful tool for doing this is the realization we are, as Glenda expresses it, "a natural variant of the human race." In accepting this fact Glenda has felt no need to understand everything. "Why was I born the way I was? I don't know. I tend to favor the prenatal theories, but the most important thing is I accept my femininity."

For SuSu femininity has made a fairly recent debut and the acceptance has grown to the level of what she calls, "the love of the feminine." This is her experience:

> *"SuSu popped out a little over a year ago and I immediately accepted and fell in love with her. I did not go through long periods of doubts, fears or guilt. To me the most important aspect of living is to love and accept the person you are and to have at least one person who likewise loves and accepts you. Feeling dignified, therefore, becomes each person's responsibility. The crossdresser can't expect to be accepted by society until she accepts herself."*

FIX WHAT IS BROKEN; ENJOY WHAT IS NOT

In Ralph Waldo Emerson's poem, BORROWING, we have a great lesson. Many times we "borrow" trouble; we think there are problems where none exist. We tend to look for the evils that never arrive. Anticipation may be the prelude to what is feared the most:

> *"Some of your hurts you have cured,*
> *And the sharpest you still have survived,*
> *But what torments of grief you endured*
> *From evils that never arrived."*

It behooves us to remember the words of the old man who said, "I am old, and I have many troubles, but most of them have never happened."

Patricia Kennedy expresses her thoughts as follows:

> *"The crossdresser must accept her condition as ever present. Little can be done to change the condition even if she wanted to change. Once this level of self-acceptance is achieved the stigmas imposed by society begin to take on less importance in the mind of the crossdresser, because she begins to see her own truth. The realization comes that she is not a pervert, a child molester or a rapist, but in fact she is like a small child who is struggling against a tide."*

Further inspection reveals she, not society, creates the obstacles. The symbolic "red flags" go up and she starts to see a real danger in allowing someone other than herself to establish her worth or value.

Patricia also believes well-established role models tend to inhibit crossdressers:

"One of the big problems here is that we were reared by parents who established sound, concise role models for each of us. Men are supposed to be men. In this role they cut grass, fix cars, carry the bride over the threshold and act in a strong, precise and calculating manner. This is the image of what we are supposed to be. While it is not totally self-imposed, it is sacred, because this is a part of our upbringing. In time I have learned that even these ideas can be overcome."

There are three factors that are essential to good mental health. They are self-acceptance, self-honesty and self-responsibility. There comes a time, possibly after seeing the "made up" face in the mirror a hundred times, the individual understands she is a crossdresser. It doesn't matter why. It doesn't matter that it violates the image of dad, son or husband, and it doesn't matter that your best friend isn't experiencing the same thing.

The honesty comes into play as the individual begins to admit she enjoys the clothes, the feelings and the relief that comes through crossdressing.

It is important that the individual analyze thoughts honestly, at least to herself. This is something that must be done continually, because the perspective will evolve, and tomorrow will bring different answers from today. The ability to be honest with self is crucial to attaining any degree of self-dignity for the transgender community worldwide.

Responsibility for self is the strength that allows each of us to do what we need to do to make ourselves happy. When one takes responsibility for our actions, there is no one else to blame. All of these factors add up to loving oneself. Once this has developed, it is easier to love other people. Self-honesty must come before we are able to be honest with others.

STOP AND SMELL THE ROSES

Once self-acceptance and self-love have been realized we are ready to move into the wonderful experience of sharing crossdressing with others. Sheri has found great joy as a member of a crossdressing organization:

"Having access to others within the crossdressing community for only the last two years, I have been elated that there is a wonderful non-sexual outlet to the drive. While trapped in a fantasy land for most of my life, I actually had little chance to grow. There was input only from my own mind games. There was a lack of factual information, even in large libraries. Little was accomplished in my move toward a satisfying experience. When the experience is centered around a sexual release, cross-dressing remains a futile experience with guilt."

Fortunately Sheri has moved beyond self-interest and self-gratification into the more fulfilling aspects of life. She can agree with Mac Davis who sang this popular folk song:

"You gotta stop and smelt the roses,
You gotta count your blessings every day,
You gonna find a rough and rocky road,
If you don't stop and smell the roses on the way."

We will find the symbolic roses when we move beyond ourselves. Theresa feels that moving into the crossdressing community and seeing how others have made dressing a plus in their lives helped more than anything else. "I hoped above all else I could reverse what had been negatives and make them into positives for my own betterment. Learning to separate the unnecessary sources of guilt from those characteristics that needed changing seemed to be the key."

Ellen also feels that the association with others in the crossdressing community has helped her to understand herself. She no longer feels guilt-ridden for the mere act of crossdressing.

SOME OF OUR CHALLENGES

When we move beyond self the joys increase, but so do the risks. I don't know many crossdressers who fail to see the challenge of it all. Let's investigate some of the challenges of moving beyond self.

GETTING ALONG WITH
YOUR WIFE OR PARTNER

Many couples consider getting along in a love relationship a daunting challenge. Adding crossdressing to the formula further complicates the relationship for many of these couples. Most crossdressers I have met tend to expect too much too soon. It is very important to give your wife or partner time to assimilate. The years of social conditioning are not easily forgotten, and these expectations contribute to anxieties, fears and resistance to the phenomenon of crossdressing.

The crossdresser should try to understand the wife or partner's point of view when she shares them. But she may hold back her real feelings in an effort to avoid confrontation or conflict. Given time, the crossdresser and partner can become more open and responsive to each other, demonstrating a willingness to compromise. Remember the pain of your wife or partner. Being married to a crossdresser is not most women's idea of happily ever after, and suppressing a part of the personality is not ideal for crossdressers.

The decision to share the femme side with a wife or partner will cause some stress. Sondra felt a tremendous apprehension. She did not know how or what to tell her. Data received clearly indicates that for most crossdressers the fear of losing the wife or partner because of crossdressing is their number one fear. Many crossdressers go through painful denial processes in an effort to spare their loved ones' feelings. (See How To Tell Your Wife, Chapter 6).

LEARNING TO PASS

As crossdressers move out of the closet, the desire to "pass" looms large. Mira wants to project a good image.

"I was browsing through the Fredericks of Hollywood catalog, but settled for a 30 ish 'standard' woman out for a day of shopping. Passing may also require the crossdresser lose weight, maintain softer skin or dress more appropriately, if she wants to effectively emulate a female."

EDUCATING CROSSDRESSERS AND THE WORLD AROUND THEM

Glenda feels that knowledge about crossdressing is necessary. She says:

"We need to understand what the whole thing is about. I always recommend that new people read four basic books: Virginia Prince's, UNDERSTANDING CROSSDRESSING; Dr. Harry Benjamin's, THE TRANSSEXUAL PHENOME-NON; Dr. Richard Docter's book, TRANSVESTITES AND TRANSSEXUALS: Toward a Theory of Cross-Gender Behavior; and Dr. Peggy Rudd's book, MY HUSBAND WEARS MY CLOTHES. I also recommend they attend a major transgender convention at their first opportunity. Living full time as a woman for even a few days is a strong growth producing experience. The association drives home the fact that one is not alone. I also recommend persons dress as much as possible and do other things considered to be womanly. It is important to develop the total personality."

Tina feels that a certain amount of knowledge is needed, since knowledge is a way of dispelling fears and insecurity. "The crossdresser needs to know she is not mentally ill or aberrant but must admit that this part of the personality exists, and begin dealing with it rather than denying it."

Mira La Cous believes the education process should move into the general public and should begin with younger people in our society:

> *"The old will rarely change. The more we do to make our children more accepting of various life styles, the more open they will be and the better society will be because of it. All of us must encourage a new view by society. We can use the three Cs: CARING, CONFIDENCE, and CHARISMA.*
>
> *I recall a newscast a few months ago in which newsmen interviewed 5th and 6th graders about what the world would be like beyond the year 2000 and what the future holds. They had many predictions including guys with longer hair who will be wearing skirts. I got the biggest smile on my face about those predictions! I believe that society is changing but not fast enough. I believe we need more movies like Tootsie. Crossdressing needs to be shown in a good light rather than as a perversion."*

Glenda Rene would like for us to instill into society the awareness that we are productive citizens and the wearing of women's clothing will not change this fact. She added, "Some males in all human cultures throughout history have had the desire to express themselves in ways that society considers feminine. What we are dealing with is a civil rights issue, but we need to raise our own level of consciousness and our own sense of dignity."

Diane describes her quest for acceptance:

> *"A single crossdresser can do little to affect society; therefore each crossdresser must deal with the issues individually. My own experience with self-acceptance was a journey accomplished very slowly over the past twenty-seven years. Even now, though willing to tolerate society, I am unwilling to subject myself to the wrath of my wife, and unwilling to subject my daughters to scorn or ridicule for having a crossdresser for a father. Until society is better educated in the issues, I may not have totally achieved self-acceptance, since I retain consideration for the opinions of*

a small segment of the public, my nuclear family."

Eileen shares her goals:

"Changing or educating society is a big goal. Changing oneself to adapt to social expectations is far simpler, but requires accepting responsibility for one's own fate. We must learn all the nuances of society's expectations for the gender we want to express. Next is learning how to conduct oneself in such a manner as to express only those elements consistent with the accepted model for that gender."

Donna Baker feels society has had an awareness of cross-dressing for years:

"When a gentleman enters Nordstrom's and nervously asks to buy the tallest pair of heels in size 12, the salesman does not snicker or ask who the shoes are for. He will say something like, 'Be sure you try them on the carpet so that you won't scuff the soles.' It's the same for the clerk at Women's World or Lane Bryant. She is very familiar with the answer, 'About my size.' To a department store phone order operator, an order from a man for one bra, one slip and one pair of panties is about as familiar as an order for one garage door opener."

Such familiarity is an evidence society is moving in the right direction. What we need to remember, however, is that while the sales persons are polite, this is probably because they make their living dealing with all kinds of people and courtesy is a part of the job. I'm not so sure about the general acceptance level. It is possible we will experience acceptance by society in our lifetime, but this should not be our dominant goal. What we must continue to strive for is self-acceptance.

Oliver Wendel Holmes summarizes this kind of tolerance:

"Every now and then a man's mind is stretched by a new idea and never shrinks back to its original proportions."

CHAPTER FOUR

THE EMOTIONAL IMPACT OF CROSSDRESSING

Aleta writes, "I have suffered all kinds of fears, suppositions, and paranoia attacks. Feelings of guilt have intensified. Why should I, a man, have all these feminine feelings?"

This statement exemplifies the feelings of most crossdressers. It seems evident the emotional issues must be addressed, since emotion is at the very heart of crossdressing. Why is there such a conflict between whom the crossdresser is and what society expects him to be? What emotional phases can the crossdresser expect as a part of the process that will lead to self-acceptance? What is the emotional impact of crossdressing?

AN URGE TOO STRONG TO BE FORGOTTEN

Aleta, like thousands of other crossdressers, has felt an emotional confrontation between whom she is and what society expects her to be. According to Aleta:

"The conflict can be very stressful. Biologically I am a male. Society expects me to act as one, yet my inner feelings are feminine. In order to survive, I have decided there is little choice but to try to fit in regardless of my true feelings. In this way I can avoid ostracism and insults by my peers, parents and other relatives. Thus, my feminine identity has been submerged deep within me.

I have become a consummate actor, often overacting the masculine role and hiding the feminine role. However, I have never been able to bury that feminine identity completely. She stubbornly lingers just below the surface until periodically released."

TRADITIONAL VIEWS

Why have Aleta and thousands of other crossdressers felt such conflict? It is related to a maze of deeply ingrained social expectations. Traditionally men have not been comfortable with emotional expression. Because of this, women, who have a wide range of emotional expression, look at their husbands, sons, fathers, and lovers with the idea that men are unfeeling creatures. Men are described as aloof, guarded, independent and guilty of distorting emotions. For example, many will show anger when they feel some other emotion such as frustration, guilt or sadness. The irony here is that many women would accept their husbands no other way except in the macho mode of behavior. Women who have been asking for men to change aren't sure they want them to.

Only within the last 20 years have women begun to be in full touch with their own emotions and life goals. Only now are they beginning to explore what they want from their men. As one might expect, there is conflict. At best many women seem ambivalent about what they want until the husband puts on a dress. At that point there are definite opinions.

In Aleta's COMING OUT LETTER, published in the Denver GIC NEWSLETTER, she explains the traditional misconception that sex and gender are one and the same. She clarifies the thoughts related to predetermined role expectations based solely upon an individual's sex and clarifies some of the theories in this way:

> *"Basically, sex is biological. Our bodies and sexual organs identify us as either male or female. Gender is our mental state, or how we identify ourselves as boys or girls and men or women. The idea that both match is a myth. There are many varying shades of gray and degrees of variance between the two. We all know women that are not very feminine and men that are not very masculine.*
>
> *If you are familiar with human biology, you are aware that the fetus contains clumps of cells that have the potential to become genitalia. For the first six weeks after*

conception, the sex of the fetus cannot be determined, then the fetus begins to form into either a boy or a girl. Only the embryo that is destined to be male receives the modifications through gestation. Should any of these miss the critical time periods or lack sufficient strength, the baby can be born genetically a male, but predisposed toward gender confusion."

This is one theory that explains the reasons for the emotional conflict felt by many crossdressers, but when they are able to break away from social stereotypes the result is usually better integrated human beings. The ability to be in touch with both masculine and feminine personality elements is important. The masculine emotions allow crossdressers to compete forcefully. Feminine feelings permit an expression of caring, compassion, joy and love. Some crossdressers are finding as contact is made with the feminine side of their personality, the range of emotional expression starts to expand. Ideally there will be an integration of these personality elements, and the end result will be an emphasis upon humanness rather than on gender. Many crossdressers over age sixty reported they had moved from uncertainty about their masculinity in their younger years to a complete integration of masculinity and femininity.

BREAKING DOWN GENDER WALLS

The breaking down of gender walls has been popularized within recent years even beyond the crossdressing community. Bill Cosby serves up an equal portion of tough and tender on the Bill Cosby Show. Alan Alda, the titular head of the kingdom of sensitive men, is still a good role model for men and young boys. Roger Staubach seems to have found the balance of courage on the playing field and a devotion to his family. Dennis Rodman, the famous crossdressing basketball player, attempts to demonstrate feminine emotions.

Christine Lavin has a song out called, SENSITIVE NEW AGE GUYS. The lyrics go something like this:

Who likes to cry at weddings?

Who thinks Rambo is upsetting?

Who tapes Thirty Something?

Who's got "Child On Board" stickers on their car?

Who's concerned about your orgasm?

Who carries the baby on his back?

The chorus answers these questions, "Sensitive New Age Guys." An emotional balance has become the topic popularized by current literature. Only a few years ago as I did research for my first took, MY HUSBAND WEARS MY CLOTHES, there were limited references to this idea. Today there are many writers joining the bandwagon. Psychologist Brian Jones and his wife, Linda Phillips-Jones, in their book, MEN HAVE FEELINGS TOO, describe the process of gaining emotional control. Read closely and you will see many correlations to the transgendered.

"Ultimately," the psychologists say, "men who have gained access to their emotions can help others learn to do it by example. Men are discouraged by their fathers, big brothers and even the women in their lives from showing how they really feel. This causes misunderstanding, because women see this as holding back. Thus, there is a communication problem as well, because men haven't learned the words for feelings." The Jones team doesn't believe that the typical male knows how to identify what he is feeling. That women fault men for their lack of expression of emotion is understandable, given women's familiarity with the emotional range. "Women put more value on feelings, talking about them and using them to make decisions," says Phillip-Jones.

Men, however, put more stock in logic. They are more likely to talk in terms of what they think instead of what they feel. That's a style encouraged by a culture that presents the ideal man, the strong and silent John Wayne or a rough and ready Rambo.

Jones writes, "We tell little boys not to cry. If they are not strong, they are wimps. The man of the nineties must resist. We are not recommending men open up and cry in the work place. That is not the place where men or women do that, but it shouldn't be inappropriate for a man to go into another man's office and share his feelings of sadness when a deal has gone awry."

Men aren't solely responsible for this failure to express their feelings. "We give them mixed signals," says Phillips-Jones. "We will say we want our husbands to open up and share their feelings. Then they finally get the courage to do it, and through facial expression or a remark, we cause them to clam up and pull back."

As an example Jones tells the story of the elderly man who, as he walked to his car in an unfamiliar neighborhood after dark, turned to his wife and admitted to being afraid. "His wife became very angry and told him in no uncertain terms that she expected him to protect them."

While women are a part of the problem, they can also be a part of the solution. In the exercises in the book the Joneses suggest men first begin to excavate their emotions while alone. The second stage leads them into a situation in which these feelings are shared with their wife or significant other.

The authors caution men to choose a time and a place in which the emotional expression is as comfortable as possible for both parties. The changes that men undergo as they become skilled at expressing themselves is sometimes a threat for the other person.

The authors stress the importance of this emotional expression. "To do otherwise. is to live life in neutral. When you stash the trash, hold in your feelings, you can't go for the gusto. You have no highs and no lows. You are unable to develop intimacy."

The key point here is that the transgender community is ahead of most in the realm of emotional feeling. The trend toward more freedom for men to express emotions may help crossdressers come to grips with their true inner feelings.

EMOTIONAL STAGES OF CROSSDRESSERS

While it is true society appears more open to men showing a

broader range of emotion, many crossdressers still seem to be "hung up" on traditional values, and total self-acceptance still eludes many. There are several very predictable emotional phases that frequently precede self-acceptance. There is no set order in which the phases occur, and there is no predetermined time frame for the phases. However, there is probably a relationship to the preconceived ideas about how life should be lived, how emotions should be expressed and how societal norms have been internalized. Once the crossdresser has worked through these emotional phases there will be a higher sense of self-worth and self-understanding.

Persons who are involved in close relationships with crossdressers, especially wives, may experience the same emotional phases. Ideally the couple can openly discuss these emotions and work through them together. For crossdressers who are not involved in a dating or marital relationship, it is helpful to share thoughts and feelings with other crossdressers. The sharing of mutual problems can be comforting, since interaction helps each person recognize the emotions that may be felt.

The extent and pattern of these emotions will vary with the individuals involved depending upon the pattern of life experiences each person brings to bear on the issue.

DENIAL

Most crossdressers I have talked with share stories about the denial of their need to dress. The denial phase is one time in which the "purge" occurs. The clothes are all destroyed, and many tell of going into the closet for a time. The expression, "Out of sight, out of mind," is a very appropriate statement. During this phase, the clothes may be destroyed or put away. Crossdressers feel it is possible to be rid of the need to dress. Meanwhile, the wife or significant other denies the complex nature of the situation. She minimizes the permanent nature of the need to crossdress by calling it a hobby. She feels that crossdressing is a condition that can be "cured" by a skilled practitioner. She may want to deny it exists. Denial is the most primitive of all defense mechanisms.

In time the crossdresser realizes cross-gender expression is not something that can be vanquished with the touch of a magic wand. Ideally the wife comes to the same realization.

HOSTILITY OR ANGER

Once we have accepted the fact crossdressing is here to stay there is a tendency for everyone involved to get very hostile. During this time, the wife or significant other becomes the enemy and from her vantage point crossdressing is the enemy. Everyone seems to be in opposition to everyone else. No one is kind, friendly, helpful or cooperative. This is the time in which a divorce may be filed or a separation may occur. Crossdressers who are single feel hostility against the whole social system that has alienated them.

Hopefully this phase will be short-lived. This is a very critical time for everyone, a time in which there is a sad mixture of self-pity on the part of the crossdresser. He continues to ask many of the same questions. "WHY, WHY, WHY? Why did this happen to me? Why do I feel so trapped by my feminine nature?"

There is jealousy lurking around every corner. The envy is directed at women, the genetic females, who are what he wants to be. This is the time that money is spent freely on clothing, wigs, makeup and all the things perceived to be necessary for the transformation into an image of womanhood.

If there is a woman in the crossdresser's life, she may be experiencing her own version of anger. Blackmail comes into play. "I won't go to bed with you until you take off that ghastly wig, and start acting more like a real man." The woman becomes bossy, demanding, rude and manipulative. She calls her mother in a fit of tears.

Moving beyond this stage is very important, since personal growth and growth in the relationship will be limited within an uncontrolled angry environment. Perhaps this poem will help:

Some thoughts sweeten,

Some thoughts sour,

Some thoughts strengthen,
Some thoughts cower,
Much of the lives of joy or pain,
Depend upon the thoughts we entertain.

FEAR

Fear is a very real and dynamic emotion felt by crossdressers and their partners and family members. The fear stage is the time for such questions as, "What will this do to our relationship? What will be the next turn of events? Where is all of this leading?" If the crossdresser is married, the wife may begin to fear escalation. She fears that what started as something rather harmless, like sharing underwear, will continue to grow to the compulsive stage or even lead to sexual reassignment surgery.

There is the fear of discovery. What will the neighbors think? What will happen if the boss finds out? Is the job safe? Is our social position safe? How will our relatives react?

Melanie and I have had our share of fears. While attending the Inaugural Ball of President George Bush, we met a crossdresser we know from the Houston area. She was dressed in a beautiful, very expensive dress. Her magical evening was made complete with the help of a male escort. It would have been fun seeing Katherine there, if we were not attending the affair with other members of our family, some of whom do not know that Mel is also a crossdresser. The fears really came alive. Could the relatives tell that she was a personal friend? Could they make the connection between the other person and us?

We had similar fears every August when we were hostesses for the Tri-Ess Chapter, Tau Chi, Luau held at our home. We frequently had more than 50 crossdressers gathered around our swimming pool. I was afraid the baritone voices would carry over the neighbor's fence. Would the neighbors hear and see our guests in the back yard? If they could, did they pick up enough of the conversation to tell what was actually happening in our yard?

The dictionary defines "fear" as the anticipation of disaster or misfortune. It is an unpleasant emotional state characterized by anticipation, pain or distress. Crossdressers are afraid reputation or life quality could be damaged because they dare to don a dress. Some call fear an intelligent foresight tempered with apprehension, dread, alarm or even panic.

Numerous crossdressers have expressed fear regarding religious issues. Is it morally wrong to crossdress? Most have reached the conclusion that harming other human beings is the greatest wrong that could occur. With this in mind it becomes important to keep the rights of others foremost.

Crystal feels the basic fears, like the ones just mentioned, are easily handled, but she feels more intimidated by personal issues:

> *"For me, there is the fear of being more addictive-compulsive. I question my own ability to handle the more encompassing nature of my desire now that I've experienced the freedom made possible by my contact with the gender community. Though sisters have warned me of the possibility of drowning in the community, I enjoy this new experience so much, I can easily imagine walking the wrong paths in my learning experience. At times I neglect other aspects of my life. I would hope that passes with time, but the capacity of finding my ultimate answer would be disastrous. My other related fear is that the answer will prove to not be satisfying. If not a transsexual, am I a transvestite who has reached or nearly reached the end of growth? Will I be doomed to a life of fantasy and parody, as neither man or woman, incapable of sharing or enjoying the relationship with my spouse?"*

GUILT

Patricia makes the following comments about guilt:

> *"Guilt is self-imposed. We beat ourselves with guilt in an attempt to change our behavior. As long as we continue to use guilt as a motivational tool we will continue to be depressed and there will be no behavior change. Words like 'should' and 'could' have no place in our vocabulary. These*

words were intended as tools to coerce children into behaving in a traditional manner. Guilt is useless and serves no master. Once a person becomes responsible for self, guilt becomes a thing of the past, a fleeting memory."

Unless a real wrong has been committed, guilt has no place in the healthy mind. If another person has been wronged, the guilt can be a constructive tool for making things right. Sometimes it is difficult to tell real from imagined guilt, or guilt imposed from the outside. Crossdressers frequently impose guilt on themselves and expect punishment and rejection.

POSITIVE EMOTIONS

When there is open communication and loving support these negative emotions can be changed into emotions that are more positive and rewarding.

Denial can be replaced with acceptance. It is important to understand acceptance does not mean understanding. There are many aspects of crossdressing I do not understand. It is similar to using the computer for word processing. I certainly do not understand computers, but accept this piece of equipment as a partner in my literary career. Probably within my lifetime there will be no clinical explanation of crossdressing, but I can accept the fact my husband has a magnificent blend of masculine and feminine emotions. Just as it is with the computer, our lives are better because of my husband's crossdressing. Acceptance has come because we have had a healthy interchange of ideas, emotions and love.

While destructive anger and hostility have been replaced by an open dialog and responsibility, there are still feelings of controlled anger. These emotions are dealt with openly and honestly. When each person feels free to discuss negative feelings, there is no desire to manipulate others.

The tendency to be judgmental is replaced with a personal responsibility for self. If a person has taken responsibility for his own life, there is little need or inclination to be concerned about the shortcomings of others. If I can be successful in keeping my own life straight this will be an effort so consuming that there will be no time to judge others! Unfortunately, a lot of criticism is based on an irresponsible desire to judge others rather than spend energy to strengthen one's own character.

Vague boundaries are replaced by clear boundaries. During the phases of negative emotions, the crossdresser does not really know where his boundaries should be. Is there too much feeling responsible for other people and the reactions of others?

Once boundaries are established, each person in a relationship can understand what they are and are not responsible for. There can be too much giving up personal identity in the name of peace. It is not good to think or feel responsible for other people, but concern for their rights is needed. The feeling of being a martyr or a victim can be replaced with a feeling of dignity and self-worth. The "poor me syndrome" is replaced with a feeling of I'm O.K. and you're O.K.

The feelings of guilt can be replaced by a sense of personal worth. It is not necessary to permit the world to inflict guilt. If each person assumes the personal responsibility for his or her actions there will be no need to accept any guilt related to our gender differences. As previously mentioned, the only valid guilt comes from harming others.

MARLBOROS OR TEARS?

A full range of emotions could be considered the gift for crossdressers. When femininity has replaced macho, there comes a license to cry. This poem from HORSES MAKE THE LAND-SCAPE MORE BEAUTIFUL says it well:

I tell you Chickadee,
I am afraid of people who can't cry.
Tears left unshed turn to poison in the duds,
Ask the next soldier you see enjoying a massacre,
If this is not so.

People who do not cry are victims of soul mutilation,
Paid for in Marlboros and trucks.

CHAPTER FIVE

BREAKING OUT OF SELF-IMPRISONMENT

The words to an old hymn give us the secret to moving beyond self-imprisonment and into a life free from many of the restraints addressed in this book:

"Truth within my conscience reigns. Be my king that I may be firmly bound, forever free."

When we are bound in truth, the keys that will free us from societal restraints are within our grasp. Truth represents the essence of moving out of a bondage in which the crossdresser sees himself as society expects him to be. Crossdressers can find freedom to move from self-imprisonment into a life filled with the joys of femininity.

"When I admitted to myself that I was a crossdresser, and stopped pretending that I wasn't one of them, whoever they are, I knew that truth had finally made me free," said Donna M. "With that degree of self-acceptance, I started exploring what was real about myself instead of a facade that wasn't real. You have to be who you are. Forget about what other folks think you ought to be."

Truth is based upon reality. The real truth is that crossdressing is not just another hobby. It is a part of life that will not go away. When crossdressers accept this fact and gain the confidence to do what is right for themselves, then they will experience freedom.

THE MEANING OF FREEDOM

The literal definition of "freedom" has many applications to the transgendered community. Look closely at the meaning and see how it might apply to you. Freedom is the state or condition of being free, but it is a package deal. With it comes some risks and consequences for thoughts and actions. Freedom is not the right to do as you want, but the liberty to do as you ought. When a person is free, he is not under strict restraint, but there is responsibility. A person who is free has the power to do, say, or think as he pleases as long as no other person is hurt.

The definition, as used in physics, is also applicable. To the physicist, freedom represents the capacity a system has for undergoing change without loss of equilibrium. Freedom emphasizes the power to make one's own decisions, impose one's own restraints, and control one's own thoughts, feelings, and actions, changing directions when necessary. As crossdressers mature many personal changes are inevitable. The wise crossdresser will recognize such changes as a healthy form of growth and maturity. Throughout the process the focus will continue to be balance and continuity.

For many crossdressers social restraints have been the force that prevented freedom. Feminine activities, interests, and needs have been suppressed. In some cases the "big secret" was hidden for many years because of fear of ridicule or rejection. It seemed easier to pretend the feminine side did not exist. This is the view of Diana:

> *"It is time crossdressers were set free instead of having to hide and be fearful of showing a major component of ourselves. Our problem relates to the fact that people try to break things down into black and white, or male and female. People are not that simple. We are born with a clean slate, and we are influenced by all of those things that happen along the way. Neither heredity nor environment alone can make us what we are, but a mixture of the two plus our own individuality will result in our unique identity.*
>
> *I personally grow more comfortable each day, but the only way this can happen is through permitting femininity to flourish. Sometimes I fear being consumed by my inner womanhood. I fear my masculinity might be lost forever. No man could handle that, but crossdressers are brought to the very edge of that experience by a desire and a yearning. I don't understand why I crossdress, but I do, and I like the experience. Every time I bring that zipper up my back I'm terrified of the thought that the zipper might get stuck. A part of me really wouldn't mind this because it is good to not have to be strong and unfeeling. But it seems like my imprisonment continues as long as the dress must come off."*

THE MEANING OF IMPRISONMENT

During the 1989 Tri-Ess National Convention in San Francisco there was a planned outing to Alcatraz. The experiences of this visit revealed the literal meaning of imprisonment. The value of freedom became real to the members who saw the massive stone walls, and felt the very essence of such separation from the world. One of the Tri-Ess members, Christy, stood on this forsaken place and pondered the meaning of it all. The prisoners had committed crimes against society, and had lost all their freedom because of those crimes. The crossdresser, on the other hand, is wronged by society, which forces him to be less than honest about whom he is. Christy saw the prisoners as people who no longer have choices, but she saw crossdressers as people who can choose to walk out of the closet or remain in their prison.

Another member, Karen, saw this imprisonment as similar to the closet. She saw it as a self-inflicted wall many crossdressers build around themselves. They can leave their closets, their symbolic prison, if they are willing to assume some risks. We can see freedom but have to be able to touch it, and to experience it. We have to be able to say, "This is who I am, and I can live with who I am. The closet can be very dark and lonely."

For the Tri-Ess members, the trip to Alcatraz reinforced the idea that so many crossdressers have been in a prison built from social expectations. Many feel they have no way out, but they do have an escape if they are willing to assume the consequences related to a more public life.

Unfortunately some feel the task of freeing themselves is not finished. Carla finds the power of eroticism incredibly strong. "I'd like to think I can control it," writes Carla. "Seeing myself as a sexual addict, I suspect if it isn't this particular manifestation, it would be another. My sexual fulfillment will maintain some of its solitary nature. While this is a morality issue, I don't view my sexual gratification as detestable as the uncaring husband. Unfortuately I remain a prisoner of my own desire."

Lana feels she has broken free of many of the problems,

including the fears of discovery or ridicule. These are overcome when individuals accept themselves. "You can't think of yourself as a freak, but as yourself." Lana feels there is still one big hurdle. "My biggest break out will be when I inform my wife, and I am unsure what the consequences will be."

THE KEYS TO FREEDOM

Something magical happened that day as the members of Tri-Ess left the prison. The boat moved away, and the image of the cold stones became a blur on the horizon. As the sea breeze lightly touched their faces, they felt free. I am told that most experienced a new commitment to move forward to a greater awareness of self and toward self-expression. Christy said, "It is liberating to break out of my cocoon - to share my identity with other people."

Christy, Karen and the other Tri-Ess members on the boat realized they held the keys within themselves to move beyond where they were. These keys are listed below:

KEY NUMBER ONE: CAMARADERIE

The trip to Alcatraz was one activity that brought the members of Tri-Ess together. There seemed to be a prevailing feeling, "Together we can conquer the world. There is strength in peer groups. It is the feeling that if others share the rejection, the pain will be minimized." Peer group interaction and support is frequently seen among teen groups. Can't you imagine one of the punk group saying, "So what if I have purple hair. You have purple hair, too. We can be laughed at together and then the very idea of being laughed at will be O.K." For the record, I'm not saying organizations for crossdressers need dress codes including purple hair. I am saying crossdressers are a very misunderstood minority, and it really helps to know other people who share the same interests, desires and inclinations. Ralph Waldo Emerson saw the value of friendship when he said, "It is not intended we all are rich, powerful, or great. It is intended we all are friends." Freedom becomes real the moment crossdressers realize they are not alone.

KEY NUMBER TWO: LAUGHTER

Shakespeare knew the value of laughter, especially when the drama of life becomes too heavy to bear. Read closely the works of this great author, and you will see moments of humor woven into the fiber of drama. He knew humor was the best way to break up tension. It is good to laugh at ourselves and to find humor even in clumsy moments as we strive, sometimes awkwardly, to achieve femininity. When appropriate, laughter is the best of medicines.

An optimist laughs to forget.
A pessimist forgets to laugh.

A word of caution should be expressed here. Sometimes humor is not an effective tool to use when dealing with other people who are trying to accept the phenomenon of crossdressing. If the person has a limited acceptance of crossdressing plus personal insecurity, misunderstandings can occur. Humor could be interpreted as insincerity. While humor is an excellent release from tension, it must be used carefully in human interactions.

KEY NUMBER THREE: SELF-DETERMINATION

What is right for me? In answering this question, one will find that self-determination is vital as crossdressers attempt freedom from stereotypes. There are many little foibles related to crossdressing that may never meet the social definition of "normal." The important thing is to find self-acceptance, by seeking out what is appropriate for you. It is important to feel an adequate degree of self-worth. With self-confidence comes the ability to make choices independent of others while maintaining concern for the interests and needs of other persons involved.

All human beings have the right of self-determination. While crossdressing is not wholly discretionary, the idea of how to reveal femininity to others can be determined by the individual. Melanie tells me there was a time early in her life when she was determined to hide femininity. She had the fear of being guilty of some wrong.

In an effort to hide the feminine traits, she compensated by getting into fights, playing aggressive sports in school and guzzling beer with the guys, despite the fact that she had no interest in these activities.

Others have said the determination to hide femininity took on the form of a "macho lingo" sprinkled with profanity, verbal abuse to women and locker room jokes. The theme here for Melanie and many other crossdressers may be a determination to fit the stereotypes of masculinity. These behaviors are good examples of the entrapment most crossdressers have experienced as they earnestly try to fit social expectations.

With self-confidence, comes the willingness to take risks, and a determination to step back from expectations and into a truthful portrayal of the feminine nature. A confident person is able to risk disapproval in order to be consistent with the true emotional makeup. Dag Hammerskjold said, "Life demands from you only the strength you possess. Only one feat is possible: not to have run away."

For one crossdresser, freedom did not occur until things got so bad, the only way to go was up. "It took the death of three friends, an illness and age anxiety to push me in the direction of self-determination."

Another said, "I've had three divorces. Need I say more?" Business failure and an attempted suicide were the catalyst for yet another crossdresser who chose to hit bottom before starting to move up. "I just called off the war inside me!" quipped Marie, who now seems content with status quo.

I enjoy meeting crossdressers who do not have to go the route of agony in search of the right to be who they are. For many the internal growth patterns are much easier and come soon enough to prevent this kind of pain. Marie assessed her own personal worth, "I just woke up one day, and discovered that I am valuable. I am a person who can be loved - even if I have a feminine side. This is not a matter of comparing myself to other men I know. There is no basis for such a comparison." Armed with this basic reality, Marie moved forward into an emotionally healthy life.

KEY NUMBER FOUR: CONFIDENCE

It takes courage to assume responsibility for oneself, particularly when there is the awareness of being somewhat different from the norm. When a person feels good about their self-image, there is less concern for what other people say or think. This is truly a worthy goal for crossdressers, one that will move the individual closer to freedom. Earlier I gave the definition of freedom as perceived by physicists who talk about the capacity for undergoing change without the loss of equilibrium. A confident crossdresser who is moving out of the closet is executing a major change in lifestyles. The degree to which confidence exists will determine the degree to which she can keep things in balance. Criticism will not throw her off, and the snickers of rude, disapproving observers will not affect her equilibrium. She is no longer under the control of the society that molded the foibles in the first place. She has the right to move, think and act as she pleases as long as other people are not hurt. She has the liberty to be herself. She is no longer absorbed by what others think about her. We should only be concerned with hostility directed to us when we start to imitate the people who are hostile.

Tere Anne, an obviously very confident person, summed it up this way, "Rude and antisocial as it may seem, you just have to say to yourself, I'm me and I want to act like the person I am. I refuse to live my life to meet artificial societal norms."

Kaplan's book, SMILES, has a poem that summarizes the need to move from social stigmas into freedom of self-will:

You are the person,
who has to decide,
whether you'll do it
Or toss it aside.
You are the person
who makes up
Your mind,
whether you'll lead
Or linger behind.

Whether you'll try
For a goal that is far,
Or be contented to stay
Where you are.
Take it or leave it,
There's something to do,
Just think it over,
It's all up to you!

CHAPTER SIX

DEVELOPING BETTER RELATIONSHIPS

One night Melanie and I sat with a group of our friends and pretended a genie had granted each of us three wishes. We shared the wishes with our trusted friends, and they shared their wishes with us. Without exception each person had at least one wish that included family. That night as the game progressed, there were a few tears shed, because when the discussion turned to matters of love, we felt a tug at our hearts. We understood the value of family members, the love expressed by family and the need to depend upon each other for emotional support. Expressions such as, "No man is an island," had a special meaning, since there were some crossdressers in the group who had never known the joy of being accepted at home. Their voices seemed an empty echo in the rumblings of a critical world. Society is sometimes an empty domain characterized by ignorance, fear and intolerance.

As I have corresponded with crossdressers from all over the world, the feeling of loneliness has been shared repeatedly. Claire expressed these thoughts:

> *"Though gregarious and usually an easy friend, I seem incapable of building a close relationship. The expression, 'if they only knew,' describes the barrier that has led me to stay at arms length throughout my later life. Until now, except those in the crossdressing community, I've revealed myself to no one other than my wife."*

Claire's feelings of being alone are real. It is tragic to not be able to share such an important part of oneself with persons you love. Above all else crossdressers long to have acceptance from the people who are important to them. Crossdressers listed concern for others as the top priority in this research.

The purpose of this chapter is to show some ways crossdressers can improve their relationships. Rich human interaction can be a replacement for voids previously experienced. The special emphasis will be upon family, since I believe accepting family members can provide a rare and much needed support.

RELATIONSHIPS OUTSIDE THE FAMILY

The large numbers of crossdressers who frequent "gay" bars give testimony to the human need to be accepted by someone or some group. The motivation to go to these bars relates to a need to interact with others. The bars are usually "safe" places where crossdressers can visit without fear, with people who sense their special needs. These persons fill the human needs of companionship. One such club in Houston is called the Palm Beach Club. This club has a mixed group, but is very accepting of the transgender community. The danger occurs when the bar becomes a "safe haven" in which personal growth or development is stifled.

Organizations for crossdressers have been very successful tools in building bridges that span the chasm of loneliness. Jo Ann has found such a group. "Since I found the crossdressing organization, I rejoice in the friendships now possible within the community."

To her dismay, Linda has found while these are wonderful friends, there is really no replacement for support found at home. She describes the situation this way:

> *"In my most important relationship, with my spouse, this new openness has proven to be a two-edged sword. We have been a very private couple. The attraction of building this ever increasing circle of friends brings its own strain. I've taken time from her to expand my experience. In this scenario any wife would feel deprived."*

RELATIONSHIPS WITHIN THE FAMILY

Full support is not always possible in love relationships, but I would like to hold this standard as the ideal, a goal worthy of our best efforts. Crossdressers who are fortunate enough to have found acceptance at home may experience the best "safe haven." In a supportive relationship self-expression occurs, and stress melts away. What better place is there to pour out the heart? Good relationships, the kind in which each person has a license to be himself or herself, are possible for crossdressers. This kind of relationship is tempered with compromise, open mindedness, and flexibility.

Each person in the relationship must define their own needs. Unfortunately people are sometimes vague about what it is they actually want from the relationship. When each person has drawn their own needs assessment, communication will improve. Somehow we all tend to forget that listening is fifty-percent of communication. We need to hear what the other person is saying, and act upon what is heard. In our own relationship, the greatest problems have come when Melanie and I did not "feel" the pain our partner is feeling. Sometimes one of us will say, "Wait! Time out! You are not feeling the hurt that I am expressing! You are not understanding how you hurt me!"

There are aspects of crossdressing family members may find distasteful. Communicate with honesty. Wives may feel confused, self-conscious about their femininity, cheated, angry and fearful. Even when it appears, the issues are under control the emotions return. Children may accept their father's crossdressing, but their response may just as likely be, "Man! Isn't this peachy?! My old man is a pervert!" There is always the risk of total nonacceptance. Hear each other out without overreacting. Unless all persons share feelings openly, there will be the shadowy areas. The unknown breeds fear, and fear breads prejudice. Relationships cannot survive long without communication.

Jaye, a crossdresser with a professional background in psychology, evaluated the effects of crossdressing upon relationships and reached this conclusion:

> *"The dressing represents such a significant element of the total self, it is difficult to factor out the clothing issue as a single entity for evaluation. I must say relationships are*

meaningful and tranquil for the people who are flexible. These people find gender expression natural since there is openness, honesty, little role playing and less posturing for people pleasing. "

HOW TO TELL YOUR WIFE

Marital relationships are a top priority for many crossdressers. If you are one of them, read the following essay carefully, and you will find answers to many perplexing questions.

A MANUAL FOR LOVE

by Jane Ellen Fairfax

How can I muster the courage to tell my wife about my crossdressing? Will she reject me, or even leave me?" These questions trouble many femmophiles. In communicating with their wives, crossdressers use a variety of methods.

How a crossdresser informs his wife directly influences the wife's response to his "woman within." Based on observed patterns of wifely response, several suggestions come to mind. Naturally, no one approach can be guaranteed to work for any given couple. My suggestions will read like a Manual for Love.

Should a femmophile tell his wife about his crossdressing? Almost always! Revealing his feminine side shows a belief in the sacred trust that is the basis of marriage. The decision to hide his femininity entails a willingness either to submerge the "woman within" or to spend much time and energy deceiving those he loves.

Submerging the feminine self, moreover, simply does not work. Mounting frustration leads to subconscious resentments, which are dumped on the unsuspecting wife in the form of unrelated quarrels. This suffering hardly seems fair to the wife, who was given no chance to either understand or accept. Thus the crossdresser may hasten the very divorce he fears will occur. It is true that informing a wife will occasionally lead to divorce. The marriage was usually in poor shape anyway. Ralph Waldo Emerson's idea of a friend was "someone with whom we can be sincere." The crossdresser's wife must be his friend.

Before sharing his feminine side with his wife, the crossdresser should have a reasonable insight into his own feminine self. Such insight may be gained by studying the works of such researchers as Drs. Vern Bullough, Richard Docter, Roger Peo, Virginia Prince and Peggy Rudd. Publications such as the Femme Mirror and Transgender Tapestry are excellent sources of information.

The crossdresser should take care to avoid certain approaches that have resulted in much grief. A wife's response is largely determined by how she learns of her husband's crossdressing. Most wives respect honesty; indeed, they are entitled to it. Some femmophiles feel it less threatening to understate their crossdressing as a mere "hobby." Perhaps it may seem so over the short term, but wives often feel deceived when feminine traits emerge that transcend the "hobby" concept. Other crossdressers simply allow their wives to discover their feminine clothes. The natural wifely reaction to this copout is to feel betrayed by her husband's "unfaithfulness." When the wife discovers that the "other woman" is really he, she feels made to appear a fool. And guess who will be the target of her resulting anger!

As crossdressers we should stress one central fact: we are more than our clothes! Far more important than the clothing is the fact that we are males who have been fortunate enough to discover a softer, feminine side to our personalities. Crossdressing, then, is simply a means of self-expression. Most women dislike the "macho" standards under which most males in our society are raised. Women tend to be sensitive and empathetic, and appreciate these traits in men. They appreciate the concept of expressing mood and self-image in what they wear. At various times, crossdressers may feel "pretty" or "sporty" or "sexy" or "outdoorsy" or "elegant', and dress accordingly. Surely it is logical for them to reject the double standard that denies men this freedom of expression.

The crossdresser should permit his "woman within" as a positive asset. For she is! Feelings of guilt, placed on crossdressers by an ignorant, hostile society, have little place in the vital process of communication between the crossdresser and his wife. How can the crossdresser possibly ask his wife to encourage "her" when he himself has trouble accepting "her"? Before revealing his feminine side to his wife, he should take note of the differences "she" has made in his life. Has "she" made him more careful of his appearance? More free to express his emotions? More sensitive and empathetic? More understanding of his wife's feelings and needs? More aware of color and beauty? Has he developed new interests and skills? Has he grown closer to God? As the crossdresser shares these assets with his wife, she will realize that her husband is still the same dear person she fell in love with and married. He has only grown.

Communication with our wives should be an exercise in empathy. Always we should strive to put ourselves in our wives' place. Fears of homosexuality or transsexuality should be dealt with honestly - as soon as possible. Concerns about children, profession and eventual goals should be explored together. Our wives are our partners. Despite our desires, our wives and families must bear the social cruelty that can come with having a crossdressing husband and father. Many wives, also, will be troubled by inner conflicts that are every bit as important as our own. Most of them did not ask to be placed into this maelstrom. It is our sacred duty to communicate with our wives, to make decisions with them, and to understand them.

Sharing our feminine side with our wives does not end with mere words. As we live our femininity, sharing continues. Rather than try to outshine our wives, we should grow with them in the feminine experience. Of course, there are some things such as menstrual cramps, childbirth, and breast feeding that we can share only vicariously. The best we can do about these biological functions is to respond in love. Unless we live full time enfemme, we may never know wage discrimination.

But we can join our sisters in fighting it wherever it exists. Being a crossdresser entails some sacrifice. We must avoid retreating into a macho double standard. Nothing seems to disgust wives more than a "man in a dress."Much more important than perfecting feminine mannerisms is developing a lively appreciation for beauty in nature, art, music, interior decorating, sewing, housecleaning, and grocery shopping. Our wives will be much more encouraging if they perceive that we are willing to buy, as far as possible, the whole feminine package.

Finally, we should remember that our wives need us as men. Everyone has heard the tired refrain of rejecting wives: "I married a man!" So many times it has been used to imprison men in society's masculine straitjacket. Yet it has a modicum of validity. We, who are more secure than average in our masculinity, should provide the masculine strength our wives need from us. That includes letting them, as far as they can, participate in the masculine side of our lives. It means being considerate husbands and devoted fathers. If we fulfill our roles as husbands, our wives will grow more comfortable with us as sisters.

EMOTION: THE BASIS
FOR RELATIONSHIPS

People are emotional creatures, and emotions have a great influence upon our lives and the lives of others. Emotions are mirrored by facial expressions and other forms of nonverbal communication. Fear, for example, will cause the crossdresser to shrink back from truth, to withhold a vital part of himself or even move back into secrecy for a time. Fear has caused wives to refuse acceptance and may result in more destructive emotions. Wives who are having difficulty with acceptance have told me the male ego in a dress is very fragile. and sometimes very hidden. This is understandable, because disparagement causes us to close the door between ourselves and those we love. I have met crossdressers who did not feel worthy to have relationships and believed they deserved rejection.

It is good to be aware of negative emotions. Most psychologists agree these must be expressed, but having done so move on to some positive emotions. Affection is a worthy emotion that can ease the pain demonstrated when negative emotions are felt. An expression of affection is a feminine quality crossdressers should develop. Most women love an affectionate husband. The wives and significant others who have adjusted best to the idea of cross-dressing say the finer feminine qualities make their husbands more lovable. They consider the demonstration of love to be a bonus factor in their marriage to a crossdresser.

ROLE MODELS

Some crossdressers have problems in relationships because of the "man in a dress," syndrome. They dress in very feminine attire but hold on to "macho" behavior and attitude. There are some role models that can be used by the crossdresser to help her relate in a more feminine way:

1. The NURTURING FEMALE is characterized by the giving of self. A mother, grandmother or nurse may provide the mental example for nurturing. Character examples of nurturing women are Florence Nightingale, Mother of the Fracchi and Marie von Trapp.

2. The WOMAN OF STRENGTH characterizes the gender female who can blend qualities of grace and charm with a demon-stration of inner strength. This is the woman who stays calm in an emergency and yet comes through as strong and helpful. Character examples are Jerosha Hale, Joan of Arc, Catherine Heathcliff and Molly Pitcher.

3. The WOMAN OF WISDOM is not that different from the Greeks of the ancient world. Such women can inspire and motivate others. Character examples are Jane Eyre and Anna Leonowens.

From these three models of the ideal woman, the crossdresser will find ideals worthy of emulation. Relationships will work better, and the Love Boat will sail more smoothly when cross-dressers demonstrate the finer feminine qualities.

FIGHT BY THE RULES

Recently USA TODAY published an article by Karen S. Peterson titled, "Fight By The Rules." Conflict in any marriage is inevitable. Unfortunately marriages of crossdressers seem especially vulnerable.

According to Ms. Petterson, how a husband handles conflict may be the key to whether a couple finds themselves in a divorce court. The article quoted Howard Markman, Professor, University of Denver, who said, "Compared to women, men seem to have difficulty handling negative emotions and conflict. Men require structure and rules. Since they were little boys, men have negotiated around rules in games. They have difficulty in handling unstructured conflict."

Markman has been studying 150 couples for 10 years to learn how to prevent divorce. He recently presented the findings of the study to the American Association for Marriage And Family Therapy. A part of the presentation included five rules for fighting:

1. Talk face to face on one topic at the time.

2. Try to understand the feelings of the other.

3. "Stop the action." Meet later if things get too hot.

4. Find a compromise.

5. Arrange a weekly "talk time" to evaluate solutions and head off fights.

These five steps are a proven remedy. I'm sure we will all agree that marriage is probably the most important event in the life of a crossdresser. Emotions run very deep. Edgar A. Guest was right when he said, "It takes a heap of livin' to make this house a home." It goes without saying, when there are problems in marriage the scars can be very deep. We all have those scars, but positive expressions of love can help us heal.

LEARN FROM MISTAKES

What we should have learned is that even the bad experiences of living can be learning experiences. I hope as each reader moves through this chapter the formula for healthy relationships will become evident. This is a goal worthy of one's best effort. Relationships must be more than feelings. There must be growth. Time is a great equalizer and a great healer. Relationship building is difficult under any condition. It is not much different from swimming up a stream, but frequently it is the conflict itself that may provide a brand-new set of water wings.

AN OUNCE OF PREVENTION
IS WORTH A POUND OF CURE

In the families of crossdressers each person tends to focus upon his own needs and expectations at the expense of others. This is human nature. We see our own vantage point better because we are so close to it. In my relationship with Melanie, I have tried to understand the agony she has felt. How does it feel to be born with characteristics labeled "different?" How does it feel to know a part of your life, a very important part, probably never will be shared fully with your parents? How does it feel to hear remarks that cut all the way to the soul? I know that Melanie has felt the darts of a society that does not understand and unjustly criticizes.

Tere Anne has shared some of her thoughts on this issue, and expressed some of the pain she experienced:

> *"There is no doubt crossdressing has a negative effect on some personal relationships. Most cannot possibly fathom the motivations of transgendered behavior. It is a totally alien idea. While my crossdressing is open with the immediate family, they still do not openly accept me as I am. It hurts when a very real and intimate part of me is rejected, considered 'sick,' and subjected to ridicule."*

Tere Anne sees this as the reason many crossdressers look

beyond family for support. "We seek the company of others similarly affected to validate that part of the personality. This further strains familial relationships. Unwarranted suspicions, fostered by ignorance and an unwillingness to understand feed on them and the alienation becomes worse."

While I understand the need for validation gained from interaction with other transgendered individuals, we have felt a need to set some boundaries in regard to these activities. We discuss whether Melanie will go to the Palm Beach Club where our transgendered friends meet or go to dinner as a couple. Within the past year we have become more open, and both of us have expressed our needs and limitations.

Melanie has tried to understand my feelings in this matter as well as in other areas, including our sexual relationship. She realizes I am not making love to a "typical" man since she enjoys sex much more when the feminine side of her personality is expressed. I remember when I was still struggling to accept the fact that for us, our lovemaking would never be "normal." Melanie tried to understand my feelings, and did so. She held me very close, and with tears streaming down her cheeks, whispered, "This is not fair to you! This really is not fair." I can tell you this understanding of how I felt moved me a thousand times closer to acceptance than anger would have moved me. We have tried to replace negative behaviors with behaviors that could best be described as positive. Neither of us has a "jelly fish spine." We stand up for what we believe to be true, but we temper these actions with respect.

Problems can be avoided if one can stay calm and objective in the face of attack. It is good to become aware of what the criticisms are. Think it through objectively so that when you are hit with it again you have formed a logical opinion. Say to yourself, "I am who I am. It is OK to be what I am. I am a crossdresser, and I can accept myself as I am." Remember anger is a normal emotion that can be constructive when handled correctly. Let off steam, but when possible do so privately so that you do not involve others in your anger. Don't expect everyone, including your spouse and family members, will always agree with you.

FAMILY REMAINS TOPS

In an ASSOCIATED PRESS article, the results of a recent survey indicated home life is still the greatest source of worry and pleasure. When I read the article I realized family relationships have the potential for providing the greatest support any cross-dresser will ever receive. On the flip side, relationships gone sour will cause the greatest amount of pain and inner conflict.

EVEN PAIN CAN HELP
YOU GROW

It is never easy to bear the pain inflicted by others. Some of it we can understand if it is caused by our own wrongdoing. Many crossdressers feel, however, all they really want is a chance to be themselves. Because of the importance of family, it is the heartfelt need of most to heal the wounds and move forward toward stronger ties. Some of our disappointments seem senseless and bewildering. There are times in which the sorrow seems to overshadow every-thing else. It is in these moments when we must remember it is in the darkest night the stars shine the brightest. Constellation follows constellation in the immensity of the magnificent universe. It is in moments such as this we should share our pain with those we love - not as in the thunder of a storm, but in the calmness of such a serene and beautiful night.

Robert Louis Stevenson said it this way, "It is friends who stand between us and our self-contempt." In our sorrow it must never be forgotten that we need other people in our life. We need bridges of appreciation if we are to cross the troubled waters of our lives. We need to be such a bridge for those we love as well. Crossdressers need to look into the eyes of those they love with compassion. It is important to be aware of the pain the other person feels when we reach out to help them.

CHAPTER SEVEN

MOVING BEYOND GUILT

The World Book Dictionary defines guilt as, "the fact or state of having done wrong, being guilty or being to blame; a guilty action or conduct; a crime; an offense; a wrong doing." These were familiar words during the impeachment trial of President Clinton. They are also familiar to crossdressers who sometimes feel less than dignified when internalized guilt preys upon both conscious and subconscious thoughts. The feeling of being less than worthy or less than "good" prompts a set of questions: What is the wrong that was done? What are the charges? What specifically is the guilty action or conduct?

Many crossdressers can honestly say, "My mind tells me I am not guilty of anything except being true to myself, but somehow there is a lack of congruence between what I know and what I feel in my heart." Most crossdressers know the boundaries between what they "should" feel and what is actually felt are blurred. The purpose of this chapter is to help clarify those boundaries, to explain why the "guilt trap" exists in the first place, and to give ideas about how guilt can be handled or dissipated. The underlying theme will be action; the momentum needed to move beyond the guilt phase into dignity. This will occur when crossdressers realize that guilt, as we know it, is a force used by society to keep people in line with standards that have been set. Thus, it behooves us to look closely at those standards and the guilt resulting from them.

Recently, Melanie and I were honored to have a very distinguished attorney, Catherine, visit with us in our home. We enjoyed discussing Catherine's career goals, since she has tried many discrimination cases. The fascination exists, in part, because our friend is also a crossdresser. Her presence in our home stimulated my imagination. I have the vision of a trial. The plaintiff in my imaginary case is society, the accuser. The co-defendants are crossdressers from around the world.

In this trial, as in all cases tried in a court of law, the defendants will have the right and the responsibility to clarify the intent of all actions for which they have been charged. Can you imagine the joy as the defendants realize the possibility of clearing charges that have been hurled for years? In our judicial system the burden of proof rests with the prosecution. The defendant is innocent until proven guilty beyond all reasonable doubt. My fictitious trial will decide the degree to which society can prove wrongs believed to have been committed by the crossdressing community.

The judge stands before the court and the bailiff speaks:

"MAY THE COURT PLEASE COME TO ORDER!"

The prosecuting attorney representing society will read the indictment counts against the crossdressers of the world. The defense attorney will present the case for the defendants. Both will call witnesses. Some of the witnesses will be family members of crossdressers, and others will be disinterested members of society. The most relevant witnesses will be crossdressers. (Personal note to my attorney friends, Catherine and Phyllis: this case is a figment of my imagination and is not intended to follow correct court procedures. As you can see, I am not ready to pass the bar exam.)

COUNT ONE OF INDICTMENT: FAILURE TO LIVE UP TO SOCIAL EXPECTATIONS

The prosecuting attorney speaks first:

"Society expects boys to be boys. When the 'blue button' is pushed, the social expectations begin. We all know that boys are not supposed to wear makeup and dresses, and are not to feel or act like girls. Even young boys who are guilty of these feelings and actions will be punished. They are sentenced to a life of ridicule as 'sissies,' and they become the object of jokes.

Boys learn at a very young age how certain things just naturally fall into the 'pink' category. To avoid ridicule, boys must stay within the 'blue' area. Some off-limit 'pink' activities include playing with dolls, crying and hugging those they love. The expected appearance, behaviors and activities for their gender must become a way of life. Thus an avoidance trap is rightfully established for anything feminine. "

The prosecution calls their first witness, Melanie.

"Did you face the embarrassing situation of being mistaken for a girl? To clarify the question further, let me ask the question another way. When you were a very young child, did people frequently say you were too pretty to be a boy?"

"Yes, and the comment was understandable, since my hair was long and curly. While at age two crossdressing tendencies were already finding their way into my psyche, the rejection of these tendencies was also growing. One fact became clear to me: long, curly hair did not belong on a boy! One day I took the scissors from the drawer, and the curls were cut off. Obviously my clumsy little hands produced a rather blotched style, but blotched hair was better than looking like a girl. "

"Melanie, are you admitting the feelings of guilt that go back as long as you can remember?" the prosecuting attorney asks.

Melanie responds, "I am saying at age two something did not feel right about being called a girl and having people say I looked like a girl."

"You admit to feelings of guilt, and yet you still dress like a girl at your age. I have no further questions."

The prosecution calls their second witness, Billie Ann.

"Billie Ann, did you also have experiences that caused feelings of guilt?"

"Yes, I did. I believe the guilt had two aspects. First, I wasn't as masculine as my peers. Secondly, I needed to make sure the difference never showed. Therefore, I spent

large amounts of time and energy making sure my attraction to feminine things was very well hidden. This resulted in what appears to be a macho resume. Since I had excluded everything that would blow my cover, only one end of the spectrum of activities was left.

A few months ago I finally realized my enjoyment of masculine and feminine things are each equally valid. In a flashback to my high school years, I remembered running out on the football field for the Friday night game. I noticed the cheerleaders and their outfits. Thirty years later I knew my desire to play football and my skills are not compromised by also wanting to be a cheerleader. "

The prosecuting attorney asks, "You say you are a man, yet did I hear you say your enjoyment of masculine and feminine things are equal?"

"That is correct," Billie Ann answered.

"The prosecution has no further questions."

The prosecution calls Theresa McGee to the stand.

"Theresa, what is your connection with the crossdressing community, and how do you feel about this social problem?"

"I am the wife of a transvestite, and my feelings are totally negative. My husband insists upon going out dressed as a woman. I have a real fear he will be picked up by the police. This would be a social nightmare for the whole family. Keeping this issue a secret has been a problem. What would the neighbors think if they found out? Since he has been involved in all this, we have no friends except for the weird ones he has met at the organization for crossdressers. I know this seems totally out of line, but he even uses the women's rest room"

The prosecuting attorney asks, "Theresa, are you saying crossdressing has proven to be a social detriment to your life?"

Theresa replied, "That is correct."

The prosecution calls Rhonda to the witness stand.

The prosecution probes, "Rhonda, are you guilty of social

wrongs?"

"I don't feel guilt, but I very strongly feel shame about being perceived as a crossdresser and about being perceived as a man who wants to do forbidden feminine things. Until recently, I've dealt with the problem by refusing to face it, but I feel isolated, worthless and alien."

The prosecution has no further questions for this witness.

The defense makes an introductory statement:

"The court must realize crossdressers did not choose to be born with a large feminine side. Their birth right is totally beyond their control. Crossdressing is the external manifestation of internal feelings and emotions. There is no social order to dictate emotional constitution. All people are not born the same. Crossdressing represents just one of thousands of social variants. There is no logic for the alienation crossdressers have felt within society. I believe, Your Honor, it is society that should be on trial. Perhaps the key issue relates to one basic truth: crossdressers harm no one. I realize a previous witness, a wife, testified about suffering from social and personal deprivation, but what harm was actually done? Is she an abused or battered wife? Is her husband unfaithful? I heard no testimony to that effect."

The defense calls its first witness, Cathy, to the witness stand.

"Cathy, what is your relationship to the crossdressing community?"

"I am married to a crossdresser. We have been married for thirty years."

"Please explain for this court how crossdressing has affected your marriage." Cathy relates:

"I have actually observed an improvement in my husband's personality when he permitted the expression of feminine traits such as empathy, compassion and love. The judgment of a prejudiced society is the real issue. It is

difficult for any crossdresser to gain social acceptance. This same perplexing problem follows many crossdressers throughout their lives.

The defense calls their next witness, Kay.

"Kay, do you believe guilt has been imposed by family and society?"

"Yes, I do. When I was very young my parents found out I had been trying on my mother's clothes. My father told me I was sick and needed help. While a woman can get by with wearing men's clothing and acting like a man, a man can't get by with doing the same thing. If a man displays feminine characteristics he is perceived to be a weirdo, a freak, or an abnormal person. I believe the guilt I feel is the result of a combination of family and society.

I have overcome this guilt, to a large degree, because I have come to realize I am a unique individual of great worth. In fact I feel that being both masculine and feminine gives me greater insight and understanding of both genders.

I am sure there are many things that have caused me to feel guilt. Regardless of what they are, I have tried to use the same approach. I identify the guilt and identify the source. This helps me understand why I feel guilty, so I can deal with it. This involves eliminating the source of the guilt or accepting it as a part of me. I try to live by the SERENITY PRAYER:

God grant me the serenity to accept the things I cannot change, the courage to change the things I can, and the wisdom to know the difference."

The defense calls their next witness, Jaye.

"Jaye, what is your role within the crossdressing community?"

Jaye answered, "I am a psychologist, and I am also a crossdresser."

The defense inquired, "Jaye, what do you perceive guilt to be within a social frame of reference?"

"Guilt is associated with not measuring up to some

standard. Internalized value concepts imposed during childhood are the most common source of guilt. A person comes into the world with little or no sense of value other than the fundamental needs as identified by Maslow and depicted at the concrete level of his hierarchy of human need. Values are taught, generally by parents and significant others, and later by peers and society. As values are internalized and a philosophy of life is developed, the person continues unthinkingly to measure self according to these values others have instilled. When the fundamental needs of the person differ from those of the instillers of values, then conflict arises. Always the person in whom the conflict arises will experience the feeling he does not measure up in some manner. The failure will be followed by guilt.

A common practice, as many of us grew up, was for our parents to control our behavior by using variations of the shame-guilt technique. I can still hear my mother's voice when I was a child asking insistently: 'What got into you? What possessed you to do that?' Invariably, this questioning was followed by the value judgment: 'You ought to be ashamed of yourself!' Then the seriousness of the value breech on my part was cemented by a liberal application of a handy switch cut from a tree, and frequently by one that I cut from the tree myself. The switch was delivered in a stance of humility to the waiting hand that would wield it with vigor until my posterior turned pink. The sting that was felt for hours served as a reminder that I deserved to feel ashamed of myself. This, in my case, was a ritual so often repeated until I became the very embodiment of shame itself."

The defense attorney asks, "How does all of this relate to crossdressers?"

"If crossdressers are perceived to be guilty, it is because the expectations of others have not been accepted at face value. Guilt results from doing an act you have been taught was wrong. I overcame guilt by realizing that unless others

are harmed there has been no wrong, even if others have defined our actions as bad. Other people have this right only to the extent that our actions affect them. What a person does behind closed doors should not be a concern to those on the other side of the door."

The defense calls Joan to the witness stand.

"Joan, who, in your opinion, determines what is right and what is wrong?"

"It becomes each person's responsibility to establish what is right and what is wrong. Persons who murder, steal, lie or rape have committed social wrongs. Guilt is valid only if one breaks the Ten Commandments or basic social values. Each person has a personal responsibility regarding such acts. Whether or not crossdressing is wrong, must be determined by each crossdresser and must be weighed within the context of not harming other human beings. While none of us can be immune to social expectations, these must filter through our own awareness of self and our own expectations of ourselves."

COUNT TWO OF INDICTMENT: MISAPPROPRIATION OF FUNDS

The prosecution calls its next witness, Mary Beth.

"Mary Beth, what is your relationship to the crossdressing community?"

"I am the wife of a crossdresser."

"Would you tell this court how you feel about money spent for your husband's crossdressing."

"I think this has gone absolutely too far. We are not rich, you know, but you could never tell it by looking at my husband. He wears designer clothes and spends a fortune on makeup and jewelry. That's only the beginning. Every month he pays dues to a crossdressing organization, and after the meeting the group goes to some gay bar for drinks

and snacks. I wouldn't be caught dead in that place, but they go every month and this gets expensive. I wish we could go somewhere as a family.

Last month our son, Tommy Don, got braces. That's another thousand dollars, and I can tell you, with this crossdressing hobby, I really don't know where the money is supposed to come from.

It has been four months since I had anything new or spent any money on myself or our children. Small chance I'll get anything in the next four months. Talk about selfish. I believe crossdressers wrote the book. "

The defense speaks:

"Mary Beth, you are correct. Crossdressing is expensive, but so are golf and race cars. I might add, so are formal teas at the country club, fancy furniture and wedding showers. You spoke about crossdressing as a hobby. While stamp collecting can accurately be called a hobby, crossdressing is not. It could best be called an investment in personal happiness, good mental health and personal fulfillment. "

The defense calls Barbara to the witness stand:

"Barbara, do you have feelings of guilt about your crossdressing?"

"I have no guilt. I feel this is a very short life span that we have on earth, and I am entitled to enjoy, in a harmless way, what pleases me most. I am not too concerned about what other people think. I also believe that crossdressing, being an attractive woman, is one of the most therapeutic things I can have in my hectic life. I have played violent pro sports. As a professional athlete there is no opportunity to compromise macho behavior, but I like the nonaggressive softness of being a woman as opposed to aggressively knocking people about. Expressing my feminine side is a welcome change and one that is providing a balance in my life. I provide well for my wife and children. Why do they want me to feel guilty? "

COUNT THREE OF INDICTMENT: WITHHOLDING EVIDENCE

The prosecution speaks:

"Many crossdressers have admitted it is wrong to keep so much of their lives hidden. Clothing is hidden, wigs are hidden and sometimes the whole truth about being a crossdresser remains hidden. Most crossdressers are honest people about other issues, but crossdressing issues are frequently an exception. Even the expression, 'I'm still in the closet,' reeks of an essence of withholding evidence. Crossdressing conventions are called 'business trips' when an explanation must be given for being out of town for several days. Being deceptive is not right, so there is a reason to feel guilty about this. "

The prosecution calls the next witness, Mr. Bob Hendricks.

"Mr. Hendricks, would you please tell this court how you are involved in crossdressing issues."

"If the charge is withholding evidence, I know of one crossdresser involved in this trial who is guilty. Recently I visited one of the local night spots here in Chicago. Almost immediately I spotted a beautiful woman in the room. I was instantly drawn to her, and I went to her table to get acquainted. Can you imagine my disbelief when she spoke to me in a baritone voice? I'm not sure what this court defines as dishonest, but I believe this is a classic example. "

The defense speaks:

"Mr. Hendricks has introduced evidence that cannot be denied. To present an illusion of being something you are not is deceptive. But wait! Crossdressers have testified that they feel feminine in their emotional composition. If this is true, and I believe it is, perhaps the crossdresser is actually being deceptive when he is in male clothing. He dresses in a suit and a tie, places a briefcase under his arm and goes off to work in a personality mood characterized by macho.

This is not his true self. This is the lie and the deception.

How can a crossdresser be totally honest? To be totally honest in crossdressing matters usually means rejection or scorn. Perhaps the secret weapon is not to internalize the displeasure expressed by others. This is a tall order when the displeasure is expressed by someone you love with your whole heart. Let's hear from another witness who sees crossdressing from a different perspective."

The defense calls Linda to the witness stand.

The defense attorney asks, "Linda, what is your relationship to the crossdressing community?"

"I am the wife of a crossdresser."

The defense attorney inquires, "Linda, do you consider your husband to be less than honest?"

"In our relationship my husband does not have to lie. We accept each other as we are. Neither of us has ever tried to hide aspects of our personalities. Honesty and trust are closely related.

But we don't trust society enough to reveal all our secrets. Therefore, we frequently attempt to hide who we are and what we do. I still try very hard not to be deceptive. When we book a Dignity Cruise, for example, our family knows that we are on a cruise with some special friends. They are always anxious to see the pictures of our trip. We make sure Donald has a few snapshots in regular attire. The family knows how much we look forward to eating lobster, enjoying the ambiance of a luxury ship, and exploring exotic destinations. No more information is needed!"

COUNT FOUR OF INDICTMENT: FAILURE AS A PARENT

The prosecution speaks:

"Society does not perceive the influence of crossdressers upon children to be healthy. Males that project femininity

are not seen as good role models. This charge is frequently tied into the previous one. It is hard to be totally honest with the children about crossdressing. Many withhold the truth in what is considered **the** *best interest of children.*

There is also the time factor. It is frequently difficult to balance time so that children are given their fair share. An absentee father is not the best kind of father. I doubt that anyone could argue this point. Time must be prioritized so this does not happen. It is wrong to place more emphasis upon crossdressing than upon the children. "

The prosecution calls Timothy to the witness stand.

"Timothy, what is your relationship to the crossdressing community?"

"My father is a crossdresser."

"Would you tell this court how crossdressing has affected your relationship to your father?"

"I no longer have a relationship with my father. Two years ago my parents were divorced. My mother told me the divorce was necessary because my dad is a sick, perverted transvestite. I've seen pictures of these guys in old issues of MAD Magazine. Can you imagine how this made me feel? My old man is a pervert. I really don't want to ever see him again. As far as I am concerned he is dead. "

The defense speaks:

"I would like to cross-examine this witness, Your Honor."

The defense attorney took one step closer to Timothy.

"Timothy, how would you describe your mother's mood when she told you about the crossdressing?"

Timothy answered, "She was very mad."

The defense inquires, "Do you really think it fair to make a judgment involving two persons when you have actually talked to only one?"

Timothy answered, "This may not be fair, but my dad is not being fair either. I don't want to discuss this with him."

"No further questions."

The defense calls the next witness, Colleen.

"Colleen, you are also the child of a crossdresser. Would you describe how your family has dealt with this issue?"

" My parents have always been honest with me. It is no surprise that they told me about Dad's special needs when I was very young. I realize this may not be right for all families, but I cannot imagine not being told about something this important. We are talking about who my father is! I feel my father is the best dad in the whole world, and it is largely because he permits the feminine qualities to be in control. "

The defense calls Annette to the witness stand.

"Annette, how has being a crossdressers affected your life?"

"Society rejects us and ridicules us. Wives and partners reject and ridicule us. We are not even acceptable to our own children. We are right up there with child molesters and rapists in terms of society's hierarchy. But that's not right, is it? We don't hurt anyone as we reach inside to get in touch with a set of values and feelings that are perfectly acceptable for persons born with a slightly different set of emotions. And yet, ironically, that same society recognizes, but has failed to deal with, the discrimination against that other group.

I usually don't deal with guilt very well. My typical reaction is to become hostile and go into some form of self-denial. That's why I am going back into therapy. I haven't learned all the answers. I may never get the answers. I try to accept the rights of others, but if I ask for something for me I am not granted my wishes. I would try to put the request into reasonable perspective. I would not want my request to interfere with or destroy the rights of others. Every time there is a conflict between my sick perverted needs and the needs of others I go into self-denial, feel guilty, and hostile. Then I withdraw. It would be far better if I could go on my way as a normal parent. This is not possible because society does not consider me normal. "

The defense speaks:

"I have observed many crossdressers who are actually better parents because they are crossdressers. Our next witness will testify to that. I call Suzette to the stand."

"Suzette, how has your crossdressing affected your relationship with your children?"

"I am a crossdresser and crossdressing became an issue in my divorce. The charge was emotional deprivation. If I had placed my needs ahead of the children, this would be a valid charge. Based upon what I feel in my heart this was not true. I got up with the babies at night, helped sell Girl Scout cookies, changed diapers and wiped noses. The children felt I was a good parent. The irony here is that when the children found out why their mother made such charges, they spent a few years trying to understand. Seven years have passed, and now they are finally realizing what a father wears does not greatly affect parenting skills. They now believe that the feminine qualities contributed to my ability to be a good father.

Recently I saw a little boy cradling a doll in his arms. He kissed the doll on the cheek and whispered a few phrases of 'baby talk' to the doll. I noticed the child and commented on the beauty of what I was observing. The child was not doing anything abnormal, because being a loving father is one of the most natural things in the world. The child was doing something human."

COUNT FIVE OF INDICTMENT: MISTAKEN IDENTITY

The prosecution speaks:

"The psychological 'high' related to experiencing femininity causes many crossdressers to feel guilty. Others jokingly say, 'I don't feel guilty until the dress comes off, and I go back to being a man.' One crossdresser even said, 'There is something about crossdressing that makes me feel

like I am disgracing women. I don't want to make fun of them, so I hope the image I portray is worthy.' There is something wrong when an activity causes this much personal disequilibrium.

Being in touch with femininity has led others to feel guilty about showing macho behaviors. As a crossdresser said recently, 'I never thought much about my temper until I let the more gentle side of me have control. Now these masculine qualities are no longer acceptable to me.' Ladies and gentlemen of the jury, what we have here are perverts, who don't know whether to feel guilty about dressing as a woman, expressing feminine emotions, or macho behavior. These people are still searching for the dominant side of their personalities."

The prosecution calls the next witness, Brenda.
"Brenda, why do you feel guilty?"

"Guilt is a major part of my life. For a long time I felt guilty because I really didn't know who or what I was. There is no longer a case of mistaken identity. I know who I am. Thankfully the basic guilt of being a crossdresser has passed. Of course that has been replaced with a new set of sins. In trying to become female, I developed a strong distaste for maleness. The callous, boorish, philandering qualities became very offensive to me. Seeing these traits in myself breeds self-hatred. This resulted in an even deeper concentration of effort to expand my feminine nature:

Am I deluding myself?
Am I to remain a man in drag?
Am I risking my life for such a little gain?
The fear that I have built a house,
based on little but my foolishness,
brings its own set of guilt."

The defense speaks:
"When given an opportunity, crossdressers are excellent

members of society. Our next witness, Ramona, will give testimony to that effect. Ramona, do you feel guilt over your crossdressing or is this an activity that brings you joy?"

"Perhaps I am more fortunate in my upbringing, but I have never felt in any way guilty about my crossdressing. It has brought me extreme pleasure and happiness. My parents never instilled any guilt associated with seeking happiness. On a similar subject I have always remained cautious about potential hazards, especially those that would affect my economic responsibility or freedom. I have carefully guarded the situations that could cause a loss of job or ruination in the professional community. This could cause hardship to my family, for whom I am responsible. I am their economic mainstay.

I manage this problem in several ways. Crossdressing is separate from my work involvement. I handled the compulsion to crossdress by finding other things that were just as fascinating. Crossdressing is limited to more private moments in my house rather than being high profile within the crossdressing community. Many of these self-imposed conditions have been satisfied now, so Ramona can have a bit more of my time and also be more visible."

The defense attorney speaks:

"Until crossdressers realize there is no case of mistaken identity, they will continue to feel guilty. Christine made this discovery after joining a club for crossdressers. I would like to call Christine to the witness stand so that she can tell about this."

The defense asks, "Christine, how did you overcome guilt?"

"There is no question I felt guilt, because I did not feel normal. It is a terrible feeling to know that the whole world thinks you are a freak, and you can't change your desires to crossdress no matter how hard you try. I did not overcome guilt until I found others who felt as I do. Now crossdressing is accepted as a part of the way I am.

It is not necessary to permit one side of the personality to override the other. The better integrated crossdressers feel they are in touch with the better qualities of both genders. They feel complete and very human. When this stage of development occurs the guilt seems to go away. "

CLOSING ARGUMENTS

The prosecution will now summarize:

"This trial has clearly indicated crossdressers are confused about their identity, are inadequate as parents and are uncaring husbands. I declare crossdressers are guilty of not living up to social expectations. Let the record show there has been misappropriation of funds. The guilt declared on this count has contributed to child neglect. It has also been proven beyond all reasonable doubt that these individuals have withheld evidence from society and to a lesser degree from those who love them. The case of mistaken identity has also been proven beyond all reasonable doubt. We have heard witness after witness tell of the costume used to masquerade as women. This is a deceptive practice that should be punished. Crossdressers have admitted they sometimes feel guilty for shopping for the feminine side of their personality. I believe spending money for their own selfish causes bring about these feelings of guilt. The brave ones that venture into department stores describe the discomfort felt when entering the women's department. It's like, 'Hey! I'm not sure that I belong here.' Others feel that family funds should be spent on the family and not feminine clothing. Let's face it. There should not be any funds appropriated for feminine edification of people with 'male plumbing'.

In a conversation with a crossdresser, Vicki, she admitted these guilt feelings. She said, 'I am divorced, and my money is mine, but I still feel guilty when I buy something for my feminine self. Something feels wrong. I think that all the clothing budget should be spent on the masculine part of my personality'.

If crossdressers admit they have these feelings of guilt, there must be something wrong. Let the record show guilt must be addressed in this court of law. "

The defense will now summarize:

"I believe the defendants are innocent on all charges. The solution for persons so troubled with guilt is to evaluate the charges. Crossdressers must evaluate the social values that imply guilt, and analyze the guilt itself. Many values must be challenged. Each crossdresser must decide which charges are valid and which are not. Once this has been done and the invalid charges are discarded the person can find freedom from the handmaiden of value judgment, guilt.

In the book by R. D. Laing, SELF AND OTHERS, the author clarifies the difference between true guilt and false guilt. 'True guilt is guilt at the obligation one owes to oneself to be oneself, to actualize oneself. False guilt is guilt that is felt when we are not being what other people feel we ought to be or assume that we are.'

We have heard testimony from crossdressers who have shared their feelings of both guilt and innocence and from family members and strangers who met crossdressers, but do not really know them personally. I challenge you, ladies and gentlemen of the jury. Listen to your hearts, and rule with equity. "

MAY WE HAVE THE VERDICT, PLEASE?

So what is the verdict? What would be your verdict if you served on the jury? If we accept the idea of Laing, we must believe a person's greatest responsibility is to himself/herself. Laing also describes the psychoanalytic term, projection. In projection people strive to induce others to become what is perceived to be ideal. If the projection is refused, a peculiar form of guilt results. For example the crossdresser's family and friends may project a role expectation. Crossdressers feel guilty because they have not become the embodiment of the other person's design. If, on the other hand, the crossdresser has become co-dependent within the relationship with the other person, a new form of guilt is introduced. There is also the guilt related to resentment that occurs when a person feels used or betrayed. This is a form of "victim" guilt.

The question of guilt or innocence must be answered within the heart. Most of us have some cause to feel we have failed ourselves or others, but it is doubtful crossdressers are as guilty as society has stated. The search for normalcy is a very strong motivator. Each person wants to find love, and sometimes they are willing to absorb guilt rather than to lose love. I am reminded of a song from a few years back that said, "I've been searching for love in all the wrong places." It is doubtful that love will be found in all the hidden voices that say, "Guys that wear dresses are bad. "

You, the people of the jury, may not be able to bring a "blanket" verdict. Some of the accused may be guilty on one count. Others may be guilty on all charges. If there can be varying degrees of guilt, perhaps some crossdressers are more guilty than others. Many are not guilty at all!

There are many lessons to be learned in this trial, but three stand above all others. First, every mistake and every guilty action will carry consequences. Second, each failure also carries the opportunity for growth. Third, if we miss the lesson, we have missed the essence of personal edification. Retire into the jury chamber which is deep within your heart, and deliberate.

When you can think of yesterday without regret,
and tomorrow without fear,
you have found true dignity.

CHAPTER EIGHT

FEAR - THE GREAT CRIPPLER

According to the stories told by my family we had a neighbor, Mrs. Wood, who may have been the most patriotic person in our town during the depression. She had a large American flag in her living room and a huge picture of President Franklin D. Roosevelt. During the thirties the President spoke frequently to the people of the United States by radio in what was called the FIRESIDE CHAT, For Mrs. Wood these indirect conversations with the President were more sacred than church. A hush fell upon her house a few minutes before the speeches began, and no person dared to move. The President had a rare gift for reaching out to America with love, understanding and compassion. He seemed to feel the pulse of the people, and he knew what their needs were. During the Great Depression, fear was the dominant emotion. To calm the people, President Roosevelt spoke these words, "All we have to fear is fear itself." He addressed his country in a clear, confident voice, and many Americans found hope in his words.

There is still a great truth to be found in what President Roosevelt said. As I have read mail from hundreds of cross-dressers, fear seems to be crippling much the same way the President's polio had been. For many crossdressers, fear is a roadblock on the path to dignity. If we look again to the words of the President, the truth will be evident. "The greatest thing we have to fear is fear itself." It will be good to look at these fears, examine each of them and search for ways to move beyond them.

FEAR OF REJECTION

Sylvia A. Voirol said, "A rainbow apologizes for angry skies." I would like to think the inner strength of many of my cross-dressing friends will be sufficient, and they will be able to forgive the angry world that rejects them. Many will move beyond fear, and self-confidence will be the positive replacement. Their success stories could help others realize they, too, can overcome fear.

It is our nature to want acceptance. The pain of rejection is probably the most prevalent pain on the face of the earth, and it is the hardest to bear. A person can live with physical pain, frustration, or even failure, but when we feel left out of the human race we hurt.

The pain felt in the human body is nature's way of saying something needs fixing. I have read accounts of persons who have neurological damage, and therefore, feel no pain. This can be very dangerous, because it is the pain that helps with the diagnosis. Does the pain we feel in rejection relate to the potential for diagnostic benefit? I believe it does.

My friend, Jaye, believes the fear of rejection is really symptomatic of some problems within the core of the crossdresser. She sees fear as an obstacle to self-acceptance and social acceptance. Here are her ideas on the subject:

> *"Much of the fear crossdressers experience about rejection is a projection of dread. The underlying psychology seems to be associated with a deep-seated conviction. The person feels their actions are wrong, inadequate or evil. Each of these negative traits will cause a self rejection, which is psychologically painful, and the pain is projected onto others. Frequently these other people really don't care, because they are so wrapped up in their own lives and don't want to be bothered with us. It is far less painful, psychologically speaking, to project rejection onto others than to admit that it is coming from inside oneself. If it is externalized, it is much less threatening and therefore more easily handled.*
>
> *It is acceptable for us to experience resentment, anger and frustration toward other people, but not toward ourselves. To admit that we really don't like ourselves is the same as admitting psychological problems. We use defensive projection and project our own defects onto other people and become angry with, and frustrated by them, instead of dealing with the core of the problem within ourselves. "*

Until the crossdresser accepts the problem as his own there will be no way to break the cycle of the rejection, pain, projection and compensation. President Roosevelt may have been right when he said. "All we have to fear is fear itself."

Jaye feels that she has personally broken the cycle. "I dug out the fears, confronted them, discovered their unfounded origins and solved the core issues. Then I discovered the fact that the fear of being rejected is greatly overblown."

Until we reach the maturity level described by Jaye, the fear of rejection can be crippling and life-destructive. It can cause us to be bitter and withdrawn. I do not believe our lives will ever be totally free of rejection. Trying to avoid it altogether may be as problematic as not looking internally for causes. Although some of it can be avoided, sometimes it will be inevitable. For example, being who you are may cause some rejection. If this is the case, the solution is to accept who you are and consider the rejection to be just one of the "thorns on your rose bush."

Follow these steps to overcome the fear of rejection:

1. Face the facts about your identity.

2. Never give in to a sense of inferiority.

3. Remember that you are a unique and precious human being.

4. Stand up for what you believe.

5. Remain unwilling to be less than the best you can be.

6. Be thankful for the characteristics that make you a blend of both masculine and feminine traits.

Kay has overcome fear in several ways. Her first step involved retirement from the Air Force:

"I retired so I could explore my sexuality without retribution. My growth as an individual helped me overcome fear. An increasing self-awareness is vital. I now know who and what I am. Personal growth is the key to overcoming fears. Growth results from knowledge gained and applied. Literature, support groups, seminars, and therapy all helped me. I have told myself that if people have trouble accepting my lifestyle then it is their problem and not mine. It is their loss because by rejecting me they are depriving themselves

of the opportunity to share friendship. "

FEAR OF TAKING RISKS

If we believe that some rejection is a natural part of life, it follows logically that some risks are involved. Frederick Wilcox said it this way. "Progress always involves risks. You can't steal second base and keep your foot on first."

Stories have been told about St. Catherine of Siena, a remarkable woman who lived in fourteenth century Italy. She may be our role model for risk taking without fear. Like crossdressers, Catherine was unconventional. Women of her time were domestic matrons, who tended to the business of home, and seldom ventured far from the hearth. Catherine bravely set forth to change the world without fear of the risk of being misunderstood. Nothing was too much a challenge for her. In her zest for life she set out to make reforms in political and social issues. This was surely unconventional for women of her culture. To help resolve these issues she learned to read and write. She wrote hundreds of letters, spoke in public about key issues and moved forward for causes. Her life became one of active contact with political rulers as well as ordinary people. St. Catherine of Siena was not afraid to take risks. Many crossdressers have seen real progress when they took that first step out of secrecy.

FEAR OF THE FUTURE

Patricia sees the fear of risk taking as tied to our fear of the future and predictable consequences for our actions:

> *"We think we know enough about the universe to predict how a given set of events will turn out. Fear is related to these predictions. Crossdressers have their set of fears, just as do construction workers or soldiers. The first step to overcoming the fear is to understand it. We should find out what is at risk and decide the nature of the fear. I have fears ranging from getting caught by my mother wearing her clothes, to telling my wife about my crossdressing. I also*

fear getting pulled over by the police while dressed. All these fears are justified, at least in my mind, yet seldom have the results turned out as badly as I might have expected. I think this is true most of the time. I have yet to tell my father that I am a crossdresser. I am afraid that he would get very upset. This is kind of funny because in a way I really don't care what he thinks. I don't like my father, but I do love him. I have decided that no good could come out of telling him, so why do it?

Let me give some background here. I am 35 years old and have been crossdressing since I was 7 or 8. I have, on occasion, ventured out into society dressed, but it wasn't until about two years ago that I put on a sweater and skirt and attended my first Tri-Ess meeting, I was stricken with fear that evening. When Nervous Nellie attended her first meeting, it turned out she had nothing to fear. I have some fears now. I am afraid that I may not be heterosexual. As my femme self I wonder how I would react to a situation with a man if he were to treat me as a woman. I am certain I would enjoy the attention. I am possibly bisexual, although I have no previous experience to back this up. I don't know how to handle this. I chose to walk my path, and I accept all that comes on the path, but I also exercise the right to fear the things on the path. "

FEAR OF BEING READ

Joan sees the fear of being read to be related to nerve, courage, and good personal decisions:

"I am a large man and could never pass except as an extremely large woman. Into the woodwork I do not fade. Since I will stand out as either a man or a woman, I have focused on wearing those elements of women's wear that I enjoy the most: earrings, stockings and high heels. I don't always wear all of them at the same time. For a while I wore Dashiki in public. Even the idea of trying to pass is slightly repugnant, but I still want to be myself. I have come to

realize that the problems that I run into are the other person's problem in response to my image.

Surprisingly if you are confident and aware of the reactions you are likely to get, other people frequently keep quiet. They do not jump to the same conclusions they might if you implicitly agreed with the typical reaction. By adjusting attitudes and behavior, hostility can be minimized. All of this would be made easier if there were more opportunities to crossdress socially with people who are supportive. It also would be easier if there could be a well-developed body of legal and administrative precedent to have ready in case there is a challenge by the authorities. The more routine and regular crossdressing can be shown to be, the less exceptional and odd."

Mira La Cous has similar fears.

"Fear of being discovered by others that know me is terrifying. I think they may have difficulty accepting what I chose to do. There is the general fear of being read by others not known to me. I personally do not enjoy humiliation as a part of crossdressing. I crossdress because it makes me feel more comfortable.

As far as overcoming my fears when I go out, I generally do not go to areas where I go in male clothes. I also do my best to pass as a standard female, whatever that is. I find that I pass very well though I am about 6'4" tall. When in male clothes I have had some people mistake me for a woman, which really makes my day. This occurs because my hair is long and permed and I have naturally soft features."

It might be of interest to crossdressers that contestants in the Miss USA Pageants are frequently very tall women. Within recent years girls have grown taller. Some of my tall friends who crossdress are confident enough to believe the attention they get relates to their attractiveness as opposed to actually being read. Phyllis says as far as she knows she has never been read, but still fears this happening. "I don't venture out unless I am fully satisfied with the way I look. It takes a great deal of time and money, and I have spent years in the closet only because I could not properly dress and was fearful of appearing in public. I had this fear of the police arresting me, losing my job and being an embarrassment to my family."

Michelle no longer has any fears associated with her cross-dressing.

"In the past, my major fear was being discovered by family, friends and neighbors. My wife knows about and delights in my ability to present my feminine side and has been a tremendous help and source of support. My older brother also knows and accepts me as feminine, primarily because he knows and loves the person under the clothes. I have also told two friends and both view it as a harmless pastime that really doesn't affect them at all. I now walk out my front door with no reservations whatever, and my basic attitude toward anyone who sees me is, 'If you don't like what you see, don't look. I am comfortable with myself and that is what counts. I would like for everyone to accept me as I am, but know that will never happen.'

Please understand, I will not stand on the roof and tell the world that I'm a crossdresser. I will also not hide this very pleasant, most important part of myself any longer. The femme side is too much a part of me to worry about what the neighbors will think. After all, I'm still the guy who mows the lawn, fixes the cars and paints the house. If neighbors, friends or family can't accept the fact that I also wear dresses, well then, they not I, have a problem. I will try to educate and inform them, if they are open-minded enough to listen, but I do not fear ostracism or snide remarks. In fact, I think fear of being found out is probably irrational.

Rather than condemnation, my experiences have been with people who express a polite form of curiosity and acceptance. They express a desire to learn more about me and the phenomenon of men who cross gender lines. I realize that this might be unusual, but I like to think that it's because I'm well informed and present a proper image when dressed."

FEAR OF LOSING YOUR JOB

Janette's fears are centered around her job:

"I am afraid every day of the week that people I work with will find out. It is the lack of tolerance that I fear. The loss of my job would bring embarrassment down upon my family. It would be instant death in my occupation if people discovered that I am a crossdresser. I am in law enforcement, a job that is considered macho. The teasing would be beyond my level of tolerance."

FEAR OF BRINGING
HARM TO THE FAMILY

Janette has other fears related to family:

"The fear I had about my wife finding out finally got to me about two years ago. I got the courage to tell her everything. Needless to say, she handled it better than I thought she would. Fortunately she loved me enough to accept the femme side! I had prayed my revelation would not cause a divorce.

About a year ago my daughter went into a drawer looking for something and found some of my femme clothing. My wife told her everything. I feared she would think of me as weird or worse. I was very happy when she accepted me for whom I am. She has not met Janette, but she has noticed that my personality has improved with the presence of my female personality."

Donna believes the only acceptance she needs to gain is from her closest loved ones, but has fears of rejection. "These fears have been confirmed," said Donna. "I must be able to resign myself to not reaching all of them."

She also says there is no fear of lack of acceptance from anyone else. "I do not need to flaunt my femme side at my workplace and my life outside the workplace is no concern to my fellow workers or anyone else."

FEAR OF LOSING AGGRESSIVE TRAITS

While many crossdressers fear the loss of aggressive traits, Patricia describes the social implications:

"The reason for the phobia relates to society's fear that a man who shows feminine traits may lose his aggressive traits in the process. Society wants a man to be boldly assertive in the building of his home. Men are seen as the protectors who will keep hostile forces away. Men are also responsible for economic concerns.

Aggression should be seen as both good and bad. A man who truly knows his masculinity and is confident in it, will accept his feminine side. Thus, he will learn all the traits needed to be a better person. With this knowledge he can stand up aggressively to hostility while demonstrating feminine qualities as well.

I was in the U.S. Army for three years and was a voluntary fireman for 25 years. When it comes right down to it, I can be as aggressive as anyone. What we must do is educate the public. People need to know we can be masculine when we must and still be feminine when we desire. Fear will not go away until this education process is complete. The fear and hatred can be overcome, but we must show ourselves in a good light as balanced people. "

CROSSDRESSING AND THE NEED FOR PUNISHMENT

Roger Peo, Ph.D, believes much fear can be overcome if crossdressers can understand how phobias relate to the need for punishment. According to Dr. Peo:

"There is usually some fear related to crossdressing. Some of it probably comes from the early days when there was a chance you would get caught and punished for this behavior. Later fear might arise from the concern that

others could learn of your behavior, costing you friends, family or your job. Sometimes this fear may become translated into heightened sexual excitement or just a general feeling of intense awareness.

In our society men are taught from an early age that they must never be like girls. Because of the awareness or knowledge, you may fail to accept crossdressing as a part of your personality. There is that subconscious rule that says you are doing something wrong. This subconscious feeling often causes the guilt that many crossdressers feel. Closely associated with this guilt is the fear that you will be caught and humiliated, yet this fear is exciting. Your adrenalin level is up and you feel good. You are in a really push-pull situation. The clothes and the image you project feel good, yet there is that subconscious feeling that you are bad and need to be punished. We were all taught that if we did something bad we would be punished, and then the slate will be clean. The rules are quickly learned and often enforced, even among adult males.

The fear and excitement are not bad. Difficulties arise when you are not aware of what is happening and allow yourself to get into situations that can create real difficulties.

Crossdressing will most likely carry some stigma in our culture. This society has much difficulty dealing with common sexual practices. When it comes to behaviors that most people do not understand, acceptance will be very slow. This lack of approval will force the average crossdresser to be cautious, to be afraid that his need will be discovered, and that discovery will cause problems.

I know that many of you would like to be free to wear whatever clothing you want, whenever you want. You are frustrated that society will not allow this behavior. Yet, our country works because we abide by a set of laws and customs, each of which limits our behavior. Consider other cultures. Do you think that crossdressers in Russia or China have an easy time or acceptance? Probably not and I suppose that penalties for such behavior would be much more severe than here. The anxiety about being discovered has both good and bad sides. In the end how you deal with it is an individual matter. "

CROSSDRESSERS SHARE THEIR FEELINGS ABOUT FEAR

Kay feels education can help us overcome fear. "Much of our fear relates to our own ignorance about ourselves and why we do what we do." Kay believes this leads to other fears including the fear of hatred, scorn and rejection. One of our young cross-dressers, Martha Rene, has the fear of being attacked by a man. "I have been taking self-defense classes." Another friend, Liz fears discrimination. She says, "The only thing I know to do is just keep plugging away, even if it means telling off the courts."

At 22, Annie has few fears. "I'm already gaining acceptance. My mother and other relatives know about me and my femme side, and I'm really not concerned about the popular views, unless someone beats me up and they haven't yet!"

Mary Beth feels most crossdressers have some paranoia, but she has felt better about the situation since living full-time in the femme role. She recommends self-confidence and self-esteem on a personal level and disregard of critical comments. Ellen agrees with Mary Beth and adds, "I believe in myself, and my fears have been overcome by this confidence."

For Sarah fear is related to social issues. "I don't care if strangers know I dress, but I do fear being identified by employers, employees, or local townspeople. Their retaliation is a reality. I do not socialize en femme with fellow employees and I have a post office box." Claire fears being alienated by loved ones. "Sometimes I wear panties, and nylons under my business suit. At home I wear only high heels and a night gown, but this causes my wife to sleep in a different room." Marge has had a similar problem. "I'm married for the second time and don't want to lose this wife, so I am careful what I do." Linda also fears rejection by loved ones and adds, "I don't want to be called a homosexual."

For every fear named by Rachel there was also a solution. Her fears are:

1. Going out. The solution: go out with your wife or partner if possible.

2. Getting read. The solution: accept it. It's O.K. Hurts just a little.

3. Shopping. The solution: Start with catalogs, and work up to the real thing.

4. Getting caught by employer. The solution. I don't know. I'm a high-ranking cop.

Arylyn says, "I fear my children will find out and exclude me from their lives." Michelle has found meeting new people helps to overcome fear. "I use mailing lists of people who are crossdressers. I have met other people in organizations for crossdressers. It is the macho image that Karen fears, "I own a shop with employees, so I must project a macho image to make it all come together." Vicki fears the situations in which she must use a lady's rest room. "This is the one situation that sets up the possibility of an arrest."

MORAL ISSUES

April puts God above all else and has worked to overcome the fear crossdressing may be morally wrong. She is diligent in the study of the Bible. Her solution for this fear is as follows: "Dig into your fears, find out the history and background of the areas you are concerned with and ask God for guidance."

Vanessa was concerned about the spiritual and moral issues raised by many people concerning crossdressing. She describes a meeting with a noted theologian, Dr. James Nelson:

"I had the privilege of meeting Dr. Nelson and mentioned to him that I was a crossdresser. I asked for his theological and personal opinion about crossdressing, and he replied, 'Transvestism is a statistical and sexual variation, but not a moral deviation.' Thus, in Dr. Nelson's informed opinion, crossdressing is neither good nor bad - only different.

The literary works by Dr. Nelson give credence to the argument that nowhere in the Scriptures does God condemn a person's psycho-social orientation. Specific sexual activities are condemned in various parts of the Bible, but it becomes evident that God has more important concerns than what we put outside our bodies. God cares what is in our minds, and our spirits. "

HOW CROSSDRESSERS HAVE OVERCOME FEAR

Table 8 of Appendix B presents a list of ways crossdressers have overcome fears. This list presents solutions for many of the fears frequently expressed by crossdressers. The remedies for fear will depend upon the nature of the emotions being felt and the unique characteristics of the individual. The list should help eliminate some of the concerns, dread, anxious thoughts and uneasy feelings that frequently go along with crossdressing.

The best cure may be in the words of the late President Roosevelt:

"All we have to fear is fear itself!"

Self acceptance is not the absence of fear,
but the conquest of it.

CHAPTER NINE

SELF-ACCEPTANCE, FIND IT WITHIN OR FIND IT NOT

"Though we may search the world over for the beautiful, we find it within or we find it not." Ralph Waldo Emerson

The key to having a rich and full life is self-acceptance, a virtue found only within. This chapter includes a provocative essay about self-acceptance. The author, Elizabeth-Ann Santini, paints a moving picture of her self-discovery. For Santini there can be no acceptance of self until there is forgiveness of self.

The last part of the chapter contains steps to self-acceptance as perceived by many crossdressers who responded to the questionnaire distributed to over 1000 crossdressers.

ON BECOMING

An Essay by Elizabeth-Ann Santini

My own personal search began in earnest in the spring of 1987. At this time I began to dig out from beneath the rubble that had piled upon my psyche since early childhood. I discovered that I alone was responsible for my evolution. Finger-pointing and blame is not only a waste of time, but they actually hinder personal growth and evolution.

I learned who I was through dealing with adversity. Learning to forgive myself and others in my life for physical and emotional pain was an important step. As a child, I passively sat back and let others push me around and ridicule my interests. I let them bury what was important to me. I later learned it is my nature to be receptive, inquiring, creative, compassionate, nurturing and intuitive. These are characteristics innate to the fully functioning female. By fully functioning I mean one who trusts her own feelings, beliefs and values and acts in accordance with these without irresponsibly accepting the beliefs of others.

For me, it was necessary to step back from the canvas of my life and systematically review much of what I had been told and to evaluate each piece of information. In turn, a decision was rendered in each case: "Is this right for me?" I kept what was valid and discarded that which I felt to be invalid.

Slowly, the cocoon unraveled and Elizabeth-Ann emerged. A caterpillar finds it rather difficult to get around and may feel worthless and may feel life is futile. But a patient, loving caterpillar who trusts her inner feelings and personal timetable, slowly builds her cocoon. Though unsure of what her future holds, she allows nature to take its course, and discovers she is a glorious creature, a butterfly! She learns that without her, there would soon be few flowers.

Even as the butterfly became a creature of beauty, you can become at peace with yourself, through your feelings, your thoughts, your actions and life itself. The Madison Avenue mentality would have us believe that we are worthless without Crest, Coors Lite, a new Toyota, or the latest Parisian fashions. Have none of it!

Reread the quotation attributed to Emerson. Happiness is not a destination. It is most assuredly a way of traveling. Throughout your life's journey, attitude is of paramount importance. Attitude is a much-maligned, often trite concept.

In aeronautics, attitude refers to the angle at which an aircraft meets the wind, whether it is level with the horizon, and whether it is climbing or descending. A pilot who is not responsible for the attitude of his aircraft is in serious trouble. In like manner, a person who does not assume full responsibility for his own beliefs, attitudes, and expectations is at the mercy of those who would sell him their beliefs. This is dangerous!

Your attitude will determine your experience, your

performance and your expectations. Dwelling on the negative aspects of a given situation: a lost job, failed relationship, poor performance, or past setbacks, automatically programs your subconscious mind to create more of the same. Mourning is our natural way to deal with loss. Allow time to grieve. Cry on a friend's shoulder over pizza or a bottle of wine. Light a candle and a stick of incense, sort out your feelings, and then let them go.

If you find yourself dwelling on these feelings of loss, seek help. That is what friends are for. That is why gender support organizations such as Transition Support in Toronto exist. Do not cry over the past. Now is the only reality.

Life is a series of nows. The manner in which you deal with each successive now will determine where you will be when tomorrow rolls around.

Your mind is more than the most magnificent, wondrous computer in existence. But with a programmer who is asleep half the time and uses a percentage of available resources the other half, it is a wonder the mind functions at all. You are the programmer. Like it or not, your computer responds precisely to the instructions you give it. Nothing just happens to you. Program in loss and setback by thinking about these continually and you will create exactly what you asked for. No more, no less. Oh, woe is me!

Thomas Edison, in attempting to find an appropriate material for the filament of the first incandescent light bulb, worked countless long hours and experimented with hundreds of different materials. Each, in turn, was drawn out into a fine strand of wire. Hundreds of times he had to return to the drawing board.

If not for his inner belief in himself and what he was doing, he might have quit and never discovered that carbon was an ideal substance for the job. Edison's own attitude may be summed up by relating an incident which occurred while he was employed at Dupont.

Working to develop a storage battery, he attempted some 350 different configurations. Each failed. One day a friend asked him about his project. How was it progressing? "Great," he replied. "We now know 350 ways not to make it." Edison knew instinctively he would be successful. He kept diligently at his work, learning from each carefully designed experiment, until he met with a desired outcome. He didn't quit after a couple of setbacks. If that had been the result of his persistence, you would be reading by candlelight.

Most of us think we are persistent, even though we may try only once or twice. Then we stop and proclaim with a sigh, "It wasn't meant to be." Persistence means keeping your objective clearly in mind and doing whatever is necessary to achieve that objective, no matter how long it takes.

When I was a child, I learned to my horror that my body, for whatever reason, was undeniably male. It has taken many years to reach this point where I am now, but my objective is lovingly etched in my mind, and it will be realized. I have overcome much as I have moved through this life, and learned an amazing amount about myself in the process.

Perhaps I would have been less in touch with what is most intimately, incontrovertibly me if I had been born in a female body to match my feminine psyche. Perhaps I would have been less of a human being. Without the struggles, I wouldn't know how truly beautiful and magical life can be.

Anyway I have a long way to go, but my clear inner vision and belief in myself and whom I am becoming makes the journey well worthwhile. As Goethe said, "Whatever you can do, or dream you can do, begin to do it. Boldness has genius, power and magic in it."

I love life, people, and most of all, myself. It is because of this blossoming self-love that I am able to share of myself and my gifts with others.

People do not behave in accordance with reality, but in accordance with their perception of reality. Radiate love, smile at everyone you pass an the street, take time to watch the sunrises and sunsets, and believe you can transcend any

challenge you face, and you will create the reality you seek.
Without growth, there is only death. Stay with your cocoon, fine-tune your perceptions and realize your inner peace. Soon you will be able to fly where you previously could but crawl. Until we meet, smile with all your being and live your reality. To the butterfly - a simple symbol of hope - in all her forms.

STEPS TO FINDING SELF-ACCEPTANCE

Perry Tanksley's book, LOVE GIFT, contains a poem with an appropriate challenge if we are to find the level of self-acceptance described by Santini.

The past unchanged remains
In spite of all regret,
And the tears we shed in shame,
Cannot make us forget.
But we can make of failure,
A stepping stone to duty,
And turn remorse into
Stairways that lead to beauty.
Then let's use past years
With all its dread and terrors
As a ladder of success.
From failure's foolish errors.

Remember these words as you apply the following steps in your own quest for self-acceptance.

STEP ONE, DISCOVER YOUR OWN VALUE

John Ruskin said, "The highest reward for man's toil is not

what he gets for it, but what he becomes for it. Even as the butterfly discovered her beauty, Elizabeth-Ann has discovered her own personal value. This is the first step in the direction of self-acceptance.

STEP TWO, ACCEPT BOTH MASCULINE AND FEMININE PARTS OF THE PERSONALITY

Accepting what Joan calls, "the seamless blend of masculinity and femininity," is a challenge for all. This is necessary for self-acceptance, personal happiness, and a sense of personal dignity.

Stephanie says, "It is important that I accept myself as I am. I also accept what things make me happy. With this I can live one day at a time."

STEP THREE, DON'T WAIT FOR UNDERSTANDING. MOVE ON TO ACCEPTANCE

Jodie is not sure self-understanding is a realistic goal, "I am constantly redefining myself and the world around me. Both my intellect and my sensory perceptions are inadequate for this task."

Kay agrees that self-understanding is beyond our grasp. She writes:

> *"I have completed a master's thesis on alternative lifestyles, but even with that knowledge I find self-understanding and acceptance do not come easily. I look at patterns of my life that may cause crossdressing behaviors. I've even forced myself to be totally male to the point of growing a beard. I've been through many purges. All of this is to no avail."*

After 50 years Rita does not understand, and after 84 years Ruth still does not understand, but both women have accepted themselves. "Crossdressing is something I like to do," writes Ruth, "It makes me feel good."

Like Ruth and Rita, Andrea is now at a point in her life when the periods of frustration have passed. "I have been crossdressing for more years than I can remember. I am now retired and have the opportunity to enjoy it."

STEP FOUR, WORK THROUGH NEGATIVE EMOTIONS

In TRANSVESTITES AND TRANSSEXUALS by Richard F. Docter, the author describes cognitive dissonance including anxiety, depression, tension, periodic guilt, and threats to self-esteem. Docter sees these negative emotions as, "associated with developing a cross-gender identity and in perceiving oneself as a transvestite." Docter explains the presence of these emotions and the relationship to social disapproval. "This discomfort and emotional tension is characteristic of the ambivalence and conflicting motivation."

It is vital for crossdressers to understand the possibility of a growth process that can move them beyond negative emotions. The realization of other persons who have faced the same conflicting motivation is comforting. This was expressed by Jenny, who described the time in her life when guilt and fear tarnished the pleasure of crossdressing. Because the negative feelings were so strong, she wished for an escape. "I had hoped I could rid myself of femme feelings, but it has helped to read books on the topic. Now I know that I am not alone." Loneliness is a negative emotion many crossdressers have faced. Knowing you are not alone is a big step in the direction of self-acceptance.

Carolyn describes the negative emotions she faced:

'The obstacle in my case was me. I let everyone else control me. I don't know if this was because I loved my family and friends or because I thought they were in need. It took me thirty years, and multiple relationships, to come to grips with myself. I have always felt good about myself, and I have been very positive, but there was this area of my crossdressing I did not accept or understand. I had to learn to put myself first occasionally. Don't get me wrong. I am

very family oriented, and love to meet my family's needs, but it got to the point I needed some understanding in return. The obstacle then became the question, 'Can I teach my loved ones to accept?' At first they seemed to accept, but then the prejudice appeared. "

Lynda Angelica Starr, who has been a crossdresser for as long as she can remember, has progressed beyond the point of feeling guilty. "I've seen so much pain and discrimination in the world that I have decided I am a very decent person. I am not hurting anyone." Lynda has sorted through guilt and has found the difference between real guilt and the guilt imposed by society.

For Sue, the guilt is more personal and not yet resolved. According to Sue, "I am just trying to figure out what's behind the naughtiness that is associated with the sex drive." The guilt related to the erotic nature of crossdressing is a major concern for many. Docter describes this as an early developmental stage. "...it is during these teenage years that the first strongly sexual links develop between fetishistic crossdressing and sexual reinforcement through orgasm." This pairing of fetishistic crossdressing and sexual satisfaction is frequently a part of the adolescent crossdressing pattern. In these cases the sexual gratification is basic to the development of transvestism. For some the phase lasts longer.

After years of guilt and torment Sarah has finally come to accept herself. "At one time I kept myself at bay by use of alcohol, a macho personality, and angry indifference directed to others. I finally realized the anger I felt was not real. It was only the product of society."

STEP FIVE, READ TO FIND TRUTH ABOUT CROSSDRESSING

Like the crossdressers previously quoted, Rene' had moments of feeling guilty, but through reading and study these feelings are being overcome:

"I finally came to realize I thoroughly enjoy crossdressing. I wanted to find out all I could about the feminine

world. My search for truth caused me to look closely at my guilt and fears. I came to realize I am doing nothing morally wrong, and if I am careful I am not doing anything legally wrong. I do still feel guilty about how it has affected my relationship with my wife, but I will continue to work on this."

STEP SIX, ASSOCIATE WITH OTHERS LIKE YOU

Many crossdressers have found support through membership in organizations for crossdressers, through computer bulletin boards, telephone calls, correspondence, participation in Dignity Cruises and meetings for crossdressers. There is something magical about the association with others who have similar interests, needs and concerns. The other people become the mirror through which self is reflected more clearly. This was the experience of Robbie who wrote, "I felt more at ease about my crossdressing. I now have supportive friends. Meeting and talking with others helps a person accept who they are."

STEP SEVEN, LOOK INWARD FOR GUIDANCE AND TRUTH

Nancy Anne feels introspection has helped her accept herself. At the same time she has come to understand what being a woman means. We live in an age in which discrimination against women still exists. "Crossdressing has made me more sensitive to women's issues." For men who want to emulate women, empathy with women is an important step in the search for fulfillment.

"Honest self-reflection, coupled with patience and prayer has helped me accept myself. I have stopped taking myself so seriously," writes Brenda.

STEP EIGHT, SEEK PROFESSIONAL HELP WHEN NEEDED

Linda found professionals who could help her accept herself."I had the usual highs and lows. There were buying sprees and purges until I finally went to a psychiatrist for help. With time, help from several types of therapy and talks with my wife, I now accept the fact of being a crossdresser."

On the other side of the coin, Anne did not find literature written by some professionals to be helpful. "Avoid the psychiatry text," writes Anne. "Look for books written by people who study crossdressing in depth; those who have participated in the experience." There are many people who do not have an adequate insight. Crossdressers should exercise caution in obtaining professional help and in the selection of literature.

STEP NINE, BE TRUE TO YOURSELF

Enid hit an element of truth when she imitated a cartoon character who said, "I yam what I yam, and that is all I yam." Linda said the same thing with somewhat different spelling:

"I gradually came to accept myself for what I am, as well as how I am. I let the girl inside me out more often, and I began to feel better about myself. The man in me is a very messy person! When the girl in me is out more often the house is a lot cleaner."

Ellen agrees. "By just being me I am a better person." Bobbie says it this way, "I like me the way I am, and I feel that crossdressing is between God and me."

STEP TEN, PERMIT YOURSELF TO FIND PLEASURE IN FEMININITY

Vicki Stone wrote, "When I look in the mirror I get a psychological high. I know of nothing that compares to the feeling I get when I am dressed and feeling feminine. !" Karen added, *"I enjoy this completely. Dressing gives me great satisfaction."*

"I know I am a crossdresser," writes Janet Marie Wolfe, "and I know I have a definite femininity. I crossdress for happiness, fulfillment, and joy."

Deborah Lyn adds, "It feels right for me. I have a need to feel feminine, and I am creatively better as a woman."

"For me to be a complete person, I must express my femininity," writes Bobbie Renee.

Linda Christine says it simply, "I love my femme side!"

Helen contributes her better qualities to the experience of being feminine."I am a better person with a wonderful feeling and glow inside. I like to reach out to all living things. I am very much in love with life."

When I asked Vicki how she has come to self-acceptance, she answered my question with another question. "Why do so many actors want to play Hamlet? It is the greatest role ever written for an actor. Likewise being a woman is the greatest role a human being can play."

STEP ELEVEN, KNOW THE NEED TO CROSSDRESS WILL NOT GO AWAY

Joan has made a profound statement. "Crossdressing will be with me forever."

Claudia found self-acceptance very simple once she understood the permanent nature of crossdressing. "I finally realized I could not change it."

Lorraine has come to terms with her need to crossdress, "And now I enjoy feeling free to be both masculine and feminine."

Expressing a strong commitment, Betty added, "Once I realized the truth, I began to work very hard at perfecting my feminine side mentally and physically."

Mechele adds, "I know it is a part of me, and it is something that will not go away. At first I thought it was just a temporary phase, but after ten years the feelings are still there. I know they are a part of me."

Becky shares the same idea. "I have admitted to myself my gender is feminine, and it is never going to change."

Aralyn discovered attempting to suppress the need causes other problems. "I get very apprehensive if I don't dress and I don't like that feeling."

STEP TWELVE, DON'T LET THE OPINIONS OF OTHERS ROB YOU OF SELF-ACCEPTANCE

"I have always accepted myself, but I realized the rest of the world did not accept me. I am on my own. In 1940 there was no name for transvestites. In 1950, 1 might have considered sex change surgery, but Christine Jorgensen went to Sweden, and I realized this was really not one of my options. I am still committed to dressing."

This quotation by Phyllis shows self-worth to be separate and apart from the attitudes and opinions of others. Cindy Lou has found acceptance, but like Phyllis, her self-worth does not depend upon it. "I have three daughters in their forties and four grandchildren. They love me because I am me."

STEP THIRTEEN, CONTINUE TO GROW

Dina said it best. "I'm still discovering some things about myself, and there's still room to grow." As personal growth thrives, good internal feelings will grow proportionally. "Wanting to dress goes back to the age of three," writes Sue. "The desire has grown through the years. I love to dress. I don't understand all of this, but I know it is very real." Claire adds, "My peace of mind grows when I can dress. Right now it is Valentine's Day, and my wife is out for the evening. I am dressed up, and I feel beautiful."

IN ALL THE RANKS OF LIFE,
THE HUMAN HEART
YEARS FOR THE BEAUTIFUL.
Harriet Beecher Stowe

CHAPTER TEN

YOU ARE
NEVER ALONE

"I felt trapped by myself and very evil. I felt my sexuality was only half fulfilled. There was a yearning to share this part of myself with someone who would understand, but I was forced to hold my secret only for myself. Under the macho veneer there was a fragile core that was easily destroyed by the slightest criticism. Fantasy became my only escape."

Susan's feelings of loneliness may sound familiar to many crossdressers. Education and public awareness will help, since crossdressers have the longing to share this very intimate part of themselves with others. I loved the response of Martha, one of the younger crossdressers we know. "After my whole family rejected me," she writes, "I joined an organization for crossdressers and found persons who understood and who actively work to educate others."

It was equally rewarding to hear the responses from crossdressers who have grown through introspection. Becky made this statement, "I am never lonely. If I get bored with myself, it seems evident I will bore others as well." Jaye wrote this comment, "I really don't experience loneliness. I enjoy solitude and am rarely lonely. I enjoy people, but I am not at all dependent on the presence of, or the association with, other people to find happiness and peacefulness inside."

The fortunate people who have found inner peace described by Jaye share these qualities:

1. They have overcome feelings of perversion, mental illness and abnormality if these feelings ever existed.

2. Each feels a personal responsibility for self that is separate and apart from the responsibilities for others.

3. The pleasure of solitude is greater than the voids described by lonely people.

4. Many have found a set of key supporters, through family or organizations, in which feelings can be shared from time to time. Most have said, however, the support groups, friends, and families do not replace quality times of introspection.

5.Good literature has supplied information about self-identity.

6. Correspondence, computer bulletin boards, telephone calls, and other forms of communication have opened doors for crossdressers to reach out to others who still feel alone.

NATURE ABHORS A VACUUM

One of the first concepts taught in general science is that nature abhors a vacuum. A cup half full of water is also half full of air. In an electrical circuit the electrons move from a point of excess to a point of deficiency. Because of this law of science, I planted honeysuckle all across the back side of our oversized lot. I knew an empty space invited weeds.

If natural laws prevail in chemistry and botany, they certainly have an impact upon human life as well. If we fail to fill our minds and hearts with positive thoughts the space will be filled with negative thoughts. Every right-minded person must will to live fully, and plunge into the stream of life. A cynic stands on the bank and fears the swirling tides below. He feels wronged when the swirling waters pull him in. A constructive person builds dams to control the waters. As long as life is empty there is no chance for self-fulfillment, dreams, or love. The creative, constructive mind is seldom a lonely mind.

LET THE WOUNDS HEAL

T.S. Elliot wrote these words about loneliness in THE ELDER STATESMAN:

"Oh loneliness,
Everybody knows what that's like,
Your loneliness is so cozy, warm, and padded,

You're not isolated, only insulated.

It's only when you come to see that you have lost yourself,
And you are quite alone. "

We do not want to lose ourselves in self-pity, fear, guilt and remorse. Such emotions are self-defeating and harmful. When left to flourish, negative emotions are the real enemies to the process of overcoming loneliness.

In Margaret Mitchell's novel, GONE WITH THE WIND, Grandma Fontaine talked about the bitter experiences of the war. "The whole world can't lick us," she said, "but we can lick ourselves by longing for things we haven't got and by remembering too much." Grandma Fontaine knew there were thousands of people who shared her heartache, but ultimately the problems were faced within her own determination. She faced the issues one on one.

Kay has felt a similar challenge and seems to agree with the author, Kate Bornstein, who wrote Gender Outlaw: On Men Women and the Rest of Us.

"I think the biggest feeling of loneliness has been despite the knowledge there are thousands more like me. I still feel no one can comprehend the way I feel. I don't feel fully male or female. I am not a part of the male population, and I am not a part of the female population. It seems sometimes the whole world is in contradiction to me. "

Even as Grandma Fontaine found answers within, Kay has looked into her own heart for solutions. "I've realized solitude is necessary. It allows me the opportunity to look inward and outward and deal with the issues influencing me. This becomes a time of renewal and growth." The old South survived the war. Kay will survive the problems she has faced as well.

John Oxenham wrote these challenging words:

"To every man there opens a way.
The high soul climbs the high way,
And the low soul gropes in the low.

And in between, on the misty flats,
The rest drift to and fro.
But to every man there opens a high way and a low,
And every man must decide which way to go. "

Our challenge is to rise above any hardship we might have. There was once a man who was half paralyzed and bankrupt. Life had become an impossible situation. This time of defeat became the moment of inspiration in which a song was written. That man was George Frederick Handel. The song was the HALLELUJAH CHORUS. It is possible to climb the high way even as Handel did. We may never compose such a masterpiece, but we can find a greater fulfillment if we find three basic personality traits:

1. self-awareness,
2. the awareness of possibilities and potential and,
3. the emotional strength within.

You can't go back and start life over and change the things you wish could be different. You are who you are. You are where you are today. The challenge is to make the most of the day at hand and accept life as you are experiencing it.

BE TRUE TO YOURSELF

Sometimes loneliness is mingled with the desire to be true to oneself. This has been the experience of Rachel:

"I do not feel lonely so much as frustrated at not being able to express my inner feelings with an external expression in the form of crossdressing. There is also a longing for feminine company. I would also like to share this part of my personality with a woman, and develop the strong loving bonds that females seem capable of forming. I would like to have a true girlfriend in every sense of the word. This is my dream"

Joan says she feels alienation and anger:

"I am angry that such a harmless activity is so misinterpreted and feared. Alienation is related to a society that is out of touch with something so fundamental it is probably running on many unexamined cylinders. I would love to meet others who would support me and my unique interest. "

It is possible to be true to ourselves if we follow five simple rules:

1. Remember to have a sense of humor.

2 Learn to be in touch with whom you are.

3. Start believing you have the freedom to express the total personality.

4. Share your guilt and fears with someone you trust.

5. Be a good listener when other people share their feelings with you.

6. Remember there are other people with similar problems.

REACH OUT AND TOUCH SOMEONE

Robert Louis Stevenson said, "It is friends who stand between us and our self-contempt." Many of you have found wonderful friends who have served as bridges of appreciation over troubled waters. Annette has found this to be true. She writes:

"Until I reached out and found others in similar situations there was no person with whom I could share thoughts and feelings. My wife would range from tolerant to openly hostile. She also pushed me into situations that forced a macho response. While I was very successful in business, a good father, and a reasonably good husband, I was repressed, hostile and lonely. I needed to express the other side of my personality, but I had not learned ways to do this. In my case there was almost a split in personality.

I have overcome the loneliness by reaching out to others with whom I can share and develop the other side of myself. I have also made a conscious effort to integrate both sides of my personality. In nonthreatening situations I can tell the truth about my true identity. "

There is thought-provoking inspiration in seeing the giant redwood trees in California. They are the largest living things in the whole world. Seeing these giants of the plant world one would assume each one to be to totally independent. This is not so. Redwoods don't have very deep root systems, thus, you will never see one growing alone. They grow in groves and their root systems intertwine. The trees actually obtain support from each other. We can draw support from each other as well.

CHAPTER ELEVEN

BEING THE BEST YOU CAN BE

"Somewhere over the rainbow,
Bluebirds fly,
Birds fly over the rainbow,
Why then, Oh! Why can't I?"

As a small child I sang this song from The Wizard of Oz. Even then the rainbow was a symbol of hope. In West Texas thunderstorms came with a vengeance. Sometimes our family drove through torrential rains. Not only was our view obstructed, but the winds seemed to force the car from side to side with an awesome force. Soon after the storm subsided and the skies turned back to a clear, crisp blue, a magnificent rainbow appeared in the sky. I could hear the rainbow whisper to me, "It's going to be O.K. Everything is going to be fine."

This book has described the symbolic storms that have clouded the lives of crossdressers, but it is not so much about storms as it is about hope and dignity. The rainbow comes after the storm. Many of you have felt a deluge of emotion; you have lost friends and family during disagreements, but you should never forget hope and dignity are real. They will come to you even as the rainbow follows the storm.

THIS IS YOUR LIFE

Some crossdressers can't see what is ahead for their lives, because they have permitted the opinions of others to be the driving force. Many have lost control of their destiny. Ideally each person will "man his own ship," take control, and become responsible for life's decisions, rather than internalize the thoughts and attitudes of others. Ideally, public opinion will present options without becoming the ultimate life script.

Jane describes the impact of social attitudes. "Some social constraints are unfair as they bridle freedom of expression for the crossdresser. For most, however, it is impractical to become free of social limitations."

It pays to listen to your heart, according to Claudia, who says, "We can treat the femme self like a person who really exists." Claudia feels we can be in contact with the girl within through analysis, self-understanding and self-realization.

Donna, a great lady in her own right, also has the distinction of being a distant relative of Ralph Waldo Emerson, author of On Self Reliance. There is a small plaque hanging over Donna's desk with these words taken from Emerson's enduring masterpiece:

> *Insist on yourself; never imitate. Your own gift you can present every moment with the cumulative force of a whole life's cultivation; but of the adoptive talent of another, you have only an extemporaneous half possession. That which each can do best none but the maker can teach him. You will always find those who think they know what is your duty better than you know it. Nothing can bring you peace but yourself. Nothing is at last sacred but the integrity of your own mind.*

In the early days of television there was a show called, This Is Your Life, which featured the life stories of famous people. The persons who had significantly affected the lives of these people were introduced, and they joined the honoree on stage. I do not remember seeing a person introduced who had a negative impact upon the honoree. The program described only those positive influences. Likewise we should internalize the influences that are good and learn lessons from the rest. As the song says, "Accentuate the positive; eliminate the negative!" During recent years numerous research studies have focused upon mental and emotional attitudes. The practice of holding onto negative attitudes will lead to the formulation of more destructive thought patterns.

REPLACE THE STORM WITH A RAINBOW

Even as the rainbow is the symbol of hope, we can find peace after the storms of life. Continue to grow. Move from the past into the present. Replacement strategies were introduced in the chapter on emotions, but should be reiterated here. To experience real self-improvement, denial must be replaced by acceptance. Anger and hostility should be replaced by responsibility. It is important to learn how to deal with our feelings and realize that manipulation by others will distort growth. Compromise in our relationships with others will help us clarify the boundaries between those persons and ourselves. We all have people who are important to us, but the value of separating their identity from our own can't be over-emphasized. This will mean we are responsible for our feelings, but we are not responsible for the feelings of others. There will be no need for self-blame when people do not accept the things about us we can not change. Likewise we can work to improve ourselves when possible. There will be no more futile attempts to change our identity in the name of peace.

Terre Anne believes the storms of life can be minimized if we live by the Golden Rule. Her formula for crossdressing with dignity includes the following:

> **1)** *"Rid yourself of the encumbrances of, 'What will they think?'*
> **2)** *Know you are an individual meriting the respect of others.*
> **3)** *Be true to yourself. Hiding who you are only lends credence to the belief that crossdressing is wrong or deviant behavior. If you feel guilty about your behavior, you have tried and convicted yourself: de facto guilty! Understand there is nothing to feel guilty about, there are few others who will overtly or publicly place you on trial to determine your guilt.*
> **4)** *Damn the torpedoes, full speed ahead!"*

What really counts is the ability to set realistic goals, according to Rebecca, who feels the importance of knowing the difference between the kind of person you can be and the kind of person you'd like to be. She describes how she has been able to continue her growth.

> *"I get better every day! The self-improvement comes*

through self-acceptance and the desire to improve. The momentum becomes a part of life. Joining organizations has helped me understand myself better, because I can see myself through the eyes of others. It is difficult to separate the crossdressing aspect of my life from the rest, so any improvement is related to the whole. In terms of self-worth I believe each person must decide for himself. If we let someone else determine our value, we will no doubt be worthless.

AS THE BLUEBIRDS FLY

In the song Somewhere Over The Rainbow, the challenge comes at the end of the song: "Birds fly over the rainbow. Why then, oh, why can't I?" It is not enough to accept the hope following the storm. We also must share the promise of the rainbow with others. I know many people who have reached out in a warm and wonderful manner. It would be possible to fill a book with stories of sisterhood, and the generous sharing of life.

Permit me to share information about one very special person, Vicki. The fabric of her life today is the very essence of caring for other people. She has reached the goal of personal dignity by extending a helping hand to others. Vicki is never too busy to assist a new sister, or to be a good listener for those with heavy hearts.

Vicki faced the dilemma of crossdressing with little or no information, yet she forged through toward self-understanding. Because of the obstacles previously experienced in her own life she seems committed to making the way easier for new sisters.

SELF-IMPROVEMENT

As Vicki reaches out to others, she shares her formula for self-improvement:

1. *Have pride in being a woman.*
2. *Remember that passing is only a yardstick of our success and should not become the reward.*

3. Accept the prejudices of others, but don't let it cloud the vision you have of your femme self.

4. In perfecting the feminine image remember to practice, practice, and then practice some more in such matters as makeup and dress.

If you follow these steps you will be able to look into the mirror and feel you are close to the desired image. But by far the greatest feeling of self-worth comes from helping others see the possibilities for their own growth and development.

History is still being written by people like Vicki who are willing to reach out to others. Theodore Roosevelt said, "There has never been a person in our history worthy of remembering who led a life of ease."

REFLECTIONS (author unknown)

When you get what you want in your struggle for self,
And the world makes you queen for a day,
Just go to a mirror and look at yourself,
And see what that girl has to say.
For it isn't your spouse, your family, or friend,
Whose judgement you must pass,
The girl whose verdict counts in the end,
Is the one staring back from the glass.
Some people may think you a straight shooting chum,
And call you a person of class,
But the girl in the glass will call you a bum,
If you can't look her in the face.
She's the girl to please, never mind all the rest,
For she's with you clear to the end,
And you have passed your most difficult test,
If the girl in the glass calls you, "friend."
You may fool the whole world down the pathway of years,
And get pats on the back as you pass,
But your final reward will be heartbreak and tears,

If you've cheated the girl in the glass.

Rene feels she continues a progressive self-improvement and lists the following steps to improving the reflection in the mirror:

1. *"Reach the point where you feel good about yourself when you are crossdressed.*

2. *Continue to learn all the makeup techniques.*

3. *Practice continually to attain a good look.*

4. *Learn about clothes and fashion. What is your proper size? What colors look best on you? How do you coordinate colors? What kind of clothing look best on you? What is the proper attire to wear at different social functions? How much jewelry is appropriate? All this knowledge must be acquired and requires continual learning to get the feeling of self-improvement.*

5. *Learn about feminine deportment. Practice walking, standing and sitting as a woman. Teaching literature is available, but nothing beats practice.*

6. *Work on voice. Nothing can make a bass voice sound feminine, but there are techniques that will make it sound softer and more acceptable. "*

Gail has found the best way to see a pleasant reflection in the mirror is by helping others less fortunate. She says, "I like to do little things to make people happy."

William Wordsworth said it this way, "The best portion of a good person's life are the acts of kindness and love."

John Holer shared these ideas, "There is no exercise better for the heart than reaching down and picking people up."

And so, my friends, we can face the world with dignity if we will first look at ourselves with dignity, and then look for ways to pass the dignity around.

CHAPTER TWELVE

RESEARCH SUMMARY

"How we feel about ourselves crucially affects virtually every aspect of our experience, from the way we function at work, in love, in sex, to the way we operate as parents, to how high in life we are likely to rise. Our responses to events are shaped by whom and what we think we are. The dramas of our lives are the reflections of our most private visions of ourselves. Thus, self-esteem is the key to success or failure."

from Braden, **HOW TO RAISE YOUR SELF-ESTEEM**

STATEMENT OF THE PROBLEM

Is it possible for a crossdresser to live a life characterized by self-esteem as defined by Braden? Is crossdressing with dignity a viable option for the crossdressing community, or is this an empty idea? What is crossdressing with dignity? Is this a social phenomenon related to winning respect and high opinion of others, or is crossdressing with dignity limited to a self-respecting character or manner as defined by Braden? Is there a relationship between personal dignity and social perceptions of the crossdressing community? Does self-acceptance increase as the crossdresser becomes more mature? Are age factors significantly correlated with personal dignity? Do the negative emotions including guilt, fear and loneliness diminish with time?

The purpose of this book has been to provide answers to these questions as they were revealed during the extensive research. This study has clarified the perceptions of crossdressers, added insight and provided new information about the status of crossdressers today.

The lack of acceptance is evident. Prejudice has distorted the lives of crossdressers despite strong evidence showing this segment of the population to be more successful and better educated than the general population.

Many crossdressers describe their personal relationships as

less than satisfactory. I have listened while crossdressers tell of rejection, frustration, and heartache. Letters have described the experience of falling to sleep on a pillow wet with tears. Friends and family members frequently refuse to accept the practice of crossdressing. A recent survey revealed the following data. Of the fathers of crossdressers surveyed, 71% were upset by the revelation that their son was a crossdresser and .01% were encouraging. Of the mothers surveyed, 54% were upset when they discovered their son was a crossdresser and 15% were encouraging. This survey conducted by ETVC indicated there is only minimal family acceptance. There seems to be a significant difference in the attitudes of fathers and mothers. While the researchers did not give a theory about this difference, I believe these data reinforce the idea that men receive a level of social conditioning greater than the social conditioning received by women.

Previous research, including the work by Bastani and Kentsmith in 1980, and Wise in 1985 examined the reactions of wives of crossdressers. These studies stressed the negative aspects of marriage to a crossdresser. Society is entrenched in an attitude of selfishness, limited by a lack of awareness, and crippled by prejudice, and perpetuated by investigating experts. It behooves us to look for a more positive side.

In an article written specifically for the primary care physician's audience of MEDICAL ASPECTS OF HUMAN SEXUALITY, April 1989, George R. Brown, M.D., described the divergent attitudes related to crossdressing in a more positive manner:

"Transvestism appears in many literary and historical contexts and has been variably condemned as a decadent indulgence, diagnosed as a perversion, revered as an enlightened transcendence of the shackles of gender, and viewed as a harmless, private hobby of men from all walks of life. Society has always held a nervous fascination for the juxtaposition of anatomy and dress as witnessed in the popularity of films such as TOOTSIE, ROCKY HORROR PICTURE SHOW, and LA CAGE AUX FOLLES, and nationally televised talk shows that repeatedly invite crossdressers as guests. "

Is it possible to transform this nervous fascination into acceptance of crossdressing? Most of the respondents to the survey believe this may happen someday, but feel the prerequisite must be an inner sense of personal dignity. Many respondents were very openly supportive of the right of society to establish norms and standards, but were equally determined to set their own personal standards that may or may not be in congruence with society. Respondents perceived a clearly defined sense of personal worth to be a more realistic ideal. This is possible only after overcoming many obstacles. Ideally the progressive self-improvement by individuals will represent a major step in the direction of social acceptance. This book has given some concrete directions for individual growth.

PROCEDURES FOR
THE RESEARCH

The FEMME MIRROR, the national publication of Tri-Ess, included the questionnaire that provided the basis for this study. The MIRROR and the questionnaire were received by over 1000 crossdressers who are members of the organization. They are heterosexual, post pubertal males. Simultaneously the research questionnaire was introduced by Jennifer Wells, the Systems Operator of the Compuserve Genderline Bulletin Board Service (BBS), and by The Outreach Institute and the International Foundation of Gender Education (IFGE). It was also listed on Carolyn's Closet BBS, Jersey Shore BBS and the Tri-Ess BBS. Many participants on the computer bulletin boards duplicated the questionnaire and distributed it to crossdressing organizations such as ETVC and Renaissance. This form of sampling broadened the base of the population. Some respondents were bisexual, homosexual, transsexual or transgendered. The majority were heterosexual.

Word of the research spread quickly throughout the crossdressing communities in the mainland United States, Hawaii, England, Germany, Australia and France. The "endless chain" approach to sampling described by Dr. Richard Docter, following his survey in 1980, also characterized this research. The wide distribution provided a very representative sampling of crossdressers. It is, however, impossible to state a percentage of responses received, since the actual number of questionnaires distributed is not known. A total of 817 responses were received prior to publication, and questionnaires were returned for years following the first printing of this book.

The format of the questionnaire led respondents to look inward for answers about their emotions and their own perceptions. The answers to the open-ended questions provided a wealth of information about the heart of the issue of crossdressing, a reservoir of data never before obtained. For many respondents, the actual experience of completing the questions forced an introspection that led to an improved self-integration.

DESCRIPTION OF THE SAMPLE

Most of the respondents were married and described themselves as members of a typical American family. Table 1 shows the marital status of participants.

Table 1. Marital status of Subjects

Married	55%
Single	24%
Divorced	14%
Widowed	07%

The average age of participants was 44.5. The median age was 45. The mean age was 45 with a standard deviation of 11.8. The range was 19 to 87 years of age.

Table 2. Age Distribution of Subjects

Under 30	02%
30-40	16%
41-50	49%
51-60	24%
61 and Over	09%

Table 3. Occupational Profile of Participants

The occupational profile seemed tilted heavily in the direction of professional persons. The percentage of retired participants was greater than the percentage of retired persons in the general population.

Disabled or retired	16%
Student	04%
Professional	39%
Skilled Worker	11%
Sales related	05%
Management	12%
Government or military	04%
Self employed	09%

The provocative nature of the questionnaire may have resulted in sampling errors. People capable of deep thought and introspection were drawn to this research. This may have tilted the population in the direction of the more highly motivated individuals. Data were obtained from the US Census Bureau regarding the educational attainment of the general population. Table 4 compares the population used in this study to the general population.

Table 4. Comparison of Educational Attainment Between the General Population and the Research Population

	General	Research
	Population	
1. Completed high school	73.0%	99.0%
2. One or more years of college	35.0%	88.1%
3. Four or more years of college	19.0%	45.0%
4. Doctoral	01.0%	08.0%

These data capture one basic truth. While society has not accepted crossdressing as a dignified activity, the population of crossdressers participating in this research has a higher educational profile that the general population.

ANALYTICAL TECHNIQUE

The hypothesis tested in this study stated that the age of crossdressers will be significantly differentiable based upon responses to the DIGNITY QUESTIONNAIRE. In the early phases of testing this hypothesis, the positive factors were listed. These included 1) self-acceptance and 2) the experience of overcoming guilt, fear and loneliness. The negative factors were listed. These included 1) a feeling of bondage related to social stigmas associated with crossdressing and 2) feelings of fear, guilt, and loneliness. The responses were converted to percentages for each of the variables based upon data received for each age group designation. Tables showing these percentages may be found in Appendix B.

The next step in the computation of a discriminate function equation involved determining whether the predictor variables, the negative and positive factors, could differentiate between the criterion groups as designated by the age of the respondent. A mean score of each predictor variable was computed by averaging the percentages for the respondents by age designation.

The degree of correlation was tested using the discriminate analysis. The discriminating power of the predictor variables, the positive factors and the negative factors, was computed using the Wilk's Lambda. The effectiveness of the discrimination was significant ($X2=p<.05$).

The greatest point of interest relates to the patterns established by the statistical analysis. There was a high positive correlation between positive factors and an older age of the participant. There was a high positive correlation between the negative factors and a younger age of the participant.

FINDINGS, CONCLUSIONS AND IMPLICATIONS

Based upon these statistical findings, we can conclude dignity is a factor of age that involves a personal growth process. Respondents to the questionnaire indicated self-acceptance is of much greater importance than acceptance by other persons. Furthermore, self-love was shown to be a prerequisite for the love of others. This study indicated a series of steps leading to the dignified life. These are as follows:

DIGNITY BEGINS WITH SELF-ACCEPTANCE

Acceptance by others is difficult, and sometimes impossible, without self-acceptance. Likewise, one cannot expect to be perceived as dignified (by others) until the self-perception reflects dignity. This process takes time, sometimes many years. The process of obtaining self-acceptance moves in a systematic, progressive manner. Based upon the data obtained in this research, self-acceptance appears to parallel Dr. Richard Docter's FIVE - STAGE THEORY OF TRANSVESTISM. (p.201 of TRANS-VESTITES AND TRANSSEXUALS). According to Docter, "We assume that transvestism and secondary transvestism represent the product of extensive change and development across the life of the individual, and therefore a developmental or life span view is imperative to understanding this behavior."

The data presented here represent a summary of information received in this study: Crossdressers listing their age as less than thirty frequently indicated a lack of self-acceptance. Those who had moved in the direction of self-acceptance had done so only after analyzing their fetishistic behaviors and eroticism related to crossdressing. The feelings of being mentally ill or perverted had resulted in therapy for some. As crossdressers moved upward toward age thirty, complete dressing occurred, and the emphasis was upon the look of glamour in the manner of Frederick's of Hollywood. This form of beauty resulted in a feeling of self-satisfaction.

Crossdressers in the thirty to forty year age bracket found self-acceptance through interaction with other crossdressers. The emphasis during this time is upon secrecy and the fear of being totally open about crossdressing. The organizations become a safe haven in which to express femininity, learn from others, and find support. During these years crossdressers begin to see the macho behaviors in their personality as negative, and a war between the two genders continues. There is an internal conflict between their masculinity and their femininity. Some turn to God in an effort to find answers about self-identity, and most try desperately to gain family support. Most crossdressers in this age group actively seek information from the literature, from correspondence with other crossdressers, and more recently through computer bulletin boards.

Between the ages of 41 and 50 many crossdressers look in the mirror and realize they aren't "little girls" any more, nor are they capable of being "cover girls." At this time many find greater self-acceptance when the look obtained by the clothes matches the chronological age. 1 know a few crossdressers who cling tenaciously to a younger image. Some feel deprived because stages of development were missed. For example they may long to wear the typical attire of the fifties, or desire a wedding dress of white. Some very conservative businessmen may find a greater fulfillment when dressing in a flamboyant manner. As they move closer to age fifty there is a greater tendency to put this phase behind and simply "blend in" as the typical lady out for a day of shopping. Self-acceptance seems to be heightened as their femininity is expressed more naturally.

As crossdressers pass the mid-century mark, most start to realize their crossdressing is harmful to no one. The 51 to 60 age group gains courage and confidence. Most of the negative emotions such as guilt, fear, and loneliness have been resolved. This is the time of heightened self-love which is followed by a more intense love for accepting persons. Also, patience with self and patience with others continues to grow.

Almost without exception crossdressers over 61 have mastered the art of self-acceptance. These persons feel more feminine than in previous years despite a few wrinkles that refuse to be hidden. They are able to set their own standards and do so when possible. Few problems remain to be resolved, and those that linger behind are less upsetting, because a true sense of humor helps even in bad situations. The true self-value is discovered.

Self-esteem is at an all-time high. This is the time of internal growth as both genders appear to be integrated. Positive thoughts are accentuated; negative thoughts are eliminated. The older crossdresser finds self-acceptance when she realizes God loves her and made her exactly as she is. Morbid as it may seem, many participants in this age group told of the death of close friends. Even this experience is positive, since facing death accentuates the value of life. The influence of such factors as respect, retirement and long-term marriages may also contribute to the personal satisfaction that occurs at this time.

A DIGNIFIED LIFE
IS SELDOM LONELY

In this study loneliness was found to be an emotional or psychological issue rather than a social one. The symptoms listed most frequently included bitterness, a tendency to blame others for personal problems, depression, anxiety, fear of being alone, sexual indiscretion, over achieving or compulsive behavior.

Michael Krawetz, author of THE LONELINESS REMOVER (Henry Holt) categorized four types of loneliness that paralleled the responses received during this study:

1."Loneliness of the unloved." Some crossdressers reported a feeling of being unloved. Some felt totally rejected by wives, parents and children.

2. "Loneliness of the friendless." Some reported a lack of friends. They felt crossdressers have no real place in society, or they felt crossdressing activities had crowded out friendships. Crossdressers who overcame this feeling did so by reaching out to others. Some told a few close friends about their crossdressing. Others became more actively involved in the crossdressing community. The secret is to reach out to others both within the crossdressing community and beyond.

3. "Loneliness of self-repudiation." Crossdressers frequently punish themselves with messages that hurt self-esteem. The solution is to stay with people who love you until you can learn to love yourself. Crossdressing organizations are very good confidence builders.

4. "Loneliness of the frantic." Crossdressers who are frantic behave compulsively. They shop to excess or engage in crossdressing activities to the point of excluding other aspects of life. Some drink excessively. The solution is to talk to a nonjudgmental person daily, and find a support group. Many respondents said they have never felt lonely, have overcome loneliness, or they have always enjoyed solitude. Maturity seems the greatest cure for loneliness. As contentment with self grew, loneliness seems to disappear. The joy of a rich fantasy life helps many.

OBSTACLES CAN
BE OVERCOME

There are many obstacles that will hinder progress of cross-dressers as they attempt to gain self-acceptance. Respondents to the questionnaire indicated the greatest problems included doubts about their own identities, feelings of being perverted, and nega-tive attitude about their own sexuality or gender expression. These problems seem to diminish as the crossdresser develops confidence and expresses the feminine qualities within.

As the crossdresser gets in touch with the "girl within" negative macho behaviors are replaced with positive feminine expressions such as compassion, and positive masculine behaviors such as leadership. This will improve the total personality. Many times there is a very painful denial process holding crossdressers back and preventing the development of the true feminine personality or the expression of anything except "macho." Many respondents believe this is a needless conflict between the two genders. As crossdressers gain maturity they perceive their personalities to be a blend of the better masculine and feminine traits. The only elements of the total personality that should be suppressed should be negative traits. There are negative feminine traits, such as a tendency to be moody, as well as negative masculine traits, such as the tendency to be abusive. The real challenge, therefore, is to find the balance between the positive qualities of both genders.

Some obstacles listed by respondents were related to society. This included the lack of parity for women within society, social stereotypes, and prejudice. Closely related were the issues related to employees. Almost without exception crossdressers felt persons on the job could not be told about crossdressing. Others listed unfair laws as a major concern. Some gave examples of social ridicule and harassment. For many the solution rests within discretion, the development of tolerance and the ability to make wise decisions independently.

The act of sharing self with family and friends was listed by many as the best way to gain confidence as a crossdresser, but for many the act of sharing was "the beginning of the end." Some relationships were not strong enough to withstand crossdressing issues.

Many respondents said things did not improve until they personally hit bottom. For some this was the loss of a job or a broken relationship. At that point in time the crossdresser said, "The only way to go is up." They soon began an introspection and were able to see themselves as possessing real value as people.

The problems related to social condemnation, ambivalence about gender, and self-condemnation can be overcome. This may require the end of the denial process and the beginning of an honest recognition of self. It may also involve resisting stereotypes. Each person must decide what is wanted out of life. Many respondents felt communication skills must be perfected before others can accept the crossdresser as he really is.

Additional information about obstacles (how crossdressers perceive them and how they have overcome them) can be found in Appendix B, Tables 5 and 6.

LEARN TO DEAL WITH FEAR

The basic fears related to crossdressing include discovery, rejection, job security, not passing, becoming compulsive and judgment by God and man. Respondents reported having the greatest difficulty in putting aside the desire to be well thought of. It is a great challenge to learn to think independently, make decisions for self and take full responsibility for actions. Most respondents said this becomes easier once there is someone with whom they can communicate honestly about the need to crossdress and someone with whom crossdressing can be shared.

Many reported high risk situations as a cause for fear. The post office box, finding safe places to go and making contingency plans were also mentioned as ways to take away this kind of fear. Tables 7 and 8 in Appendix B deal with fear as it is perceived by crossdressers.

LEARN TO RECOGNIZE
TRUE GUILT

Many respondents reported no guilt related to crossdressing, since guilt involves committing an offense. For those still caught up in the guilt trap, the culprits seem to relate to sexual eroticism, problems related to the family, deception, failure to live up to the expectations of others and gender roles. Those respondents who have overcome guilt stressed the importance of separating real or valid guilt from imagined or false guilt. This is best accomplished by developing a self-awareness that includes an acceptance of crossdressing. Guilt should be perceived as internal rather than external.

Tables 9 and 10 in Appendix B give additional information about the crossdresser's perception of fear.

IMPROVE HUMAN RELATIONSHIPS

Crossdressers who have been able to blend crossdressing and human relationships together in a positive manner have mastered the art of communication and compromise. They have also found a reasonable balance between the masculine and feminine qualities within their personalities.

Some crossdressers reported an improvement in their relationships when negative masculine traits are replaced by feminine qualities such as an open expression of love and tenderness. In cases in which crossdressing is forbidden in close relationships, crossdressing respondents reported anxiety, nervousness or even physiological problems.

Most respondents described work relationships as totally separate from crossdressing. This is understandable, since loss of employment was listed as one of the major fears.

In most cases the "secret" is also kept from neighbors and most friends, since there is the risk of losing social respect. Many respondents described their personalities as macho. This type of behavior seems to be a safe disguise for some. The brave crossdressers who shared their crossdressing with people outside the family frequently found a lack of understanding. Some people assumed the crossdresser to be gay.

Crossdressers who have found an accepting wife or a girl-friend listed more specific examples of fulfillment and happiness. An analysis of these data revealed a high positive correlation between expressed acceptance by either a wife or a girlfriend and an expression of fulfillment by the crossdresser.

Most crossdressers who have not found a positive relationship with a woman consider life to be empty and void of fulfillment. Almost without exception this desire is the number one concern for the crossdresser.

SUMMARY

This study has examined the role of the crossdresser within a societal flame of reference. It has shown the need for a complex cultural change if crossdressing is to be perceived as a dignified activity. Such a change can occur with a strong educational program designed to replace prejudice with knowledge about gender and human variants.

Closely related to social attitude is the problem crossdressers face in relationships with friends and family. For many a life time is spent searching for answers that can only be found in love and compassion. On the other hand most crossdressers describe the general relationships, such as those with neighbors, casual friends or neighbors, to be unaffected since crossdressing remains a secret activity.

Emotional issues that surround crossdressing were addressed. Respondents consistently reported a decline of negative emotions, i.e., guilt, fear, and loneliness as they grew older. Likewise they reported an increase in the more positive emotions, including compassion, love, and empathy, as their chronological age increased. Thus, this study has shown a direct relationship between the maturity level of the crossdresser and the absence of these negative emotions and the presence of positive emotions. This conclusion was reached following an analysis of data obtained from specific age groups. Valid fears, such as rejection by friends and family, and the loss of professional standing was found within all age groups. These are considered "valid" or justifiable fears. Likewise, some forms of guilt remain throughout the lives of many crossdressers including the guilt related to harm to family members.

Self-perceptions of crossdressers were also evaluated. Data obtained suggest many crossdressers are not waiting for public acceptance. These persons are moving ahead toward self-acceptance and self-respect. Personal growth and improvement were considered valuable tools. Manifesting a life worthy of trust is considered more important than a public image, since it may ultimately help sanction the crossdresser's positive role within society.

Data obtained from older crossdressers showed this subpopulation to be independent thinkers capable of making wise decisions. These respondents described decisions affecting personal life and happiness to be separate and apart from public opinion or the opinions of loved ones.

Dignity can be found internally and externally. Ideally, a person will feel dignified and also will be perceived by others in a positive manner, but sometimes this is not possible. Lack of public acceptance has been the rule for most crossdressers. Therefore, a contentment with the "secret" life has evolved for most. The more mature crossdressers have learned not to be troubled by public disapproval. In all other aspects of life many report being perceived as dignified people. Many hold important jobs and elected offices.

This study has shown the crossdressing community to be superior in at least two ways: educational level and professional attainment. My observations have shown a population worthy of highest acclaim for being sound productive people. Eight percent of the participants in this study have earned a doctoral level degree. This compares to one percent of the general population. The percentage of professional men was also higher than the norm for each age category. The men surveyed were conventional and conservative in all areas except crossdressing.

As in the case with most people, crossdressers need praise and admiration. The interaction with other crossdressers provides a "safe" environment in which to receive positive reinforcement. Crossdressing organizations, correspondence with other crossdressers, telephone calls, and computer bulletin boards have a place in the life of the crossdresser.

In 1877 Edward Fitzgerald wrote, "Taste is the feminine form of genius," and that is an excellent summary of this study.

Every day you will paint a portrait of yourself
through the life you decide to live.
Autograph your masterpiece with dignity.

EPILOG

Sheryl Ann Taylor of California believes crossdressing with dignity is possible on a personal level.

"I believe an inner peace came when I accepted my feminine self and its role in my life. It involved acting in a responsible and mature manner. The source of this peace is internal rather than from some external stimuli. This is not to say our environment could be and should be less hostile. But we have to remember many societies require rigid gender roles which are assigned at birth. Men do this and wear that. Women do this and wear that. Thus gender determines what each member of that society will do, and clothing is the uniform of that gender. Such a separation serves the purpose of keeping society orderly or uniform. Family traditions are based upon strict gender identification. Therefore, a change of gender, however temporary or permanent, can be unsettling, and the reaction to it may be severe."

Diane of Oklahoma writes:

"I really believe that in the foreseeable future, especially in America's heartland, crossdressers can't realistically expect to be treated as ordinary people in most contexts. I would, of course, welcome a world where one is not stigmatized if one wears clothes out of normal stereotyped expectations, but I just don't see that happening. One simply must accept oneself. Assuming your crossdressing doesn't harm others and you are discreet where discretion is called for, you can be dignified on a personal level, through self-understanding."

Jessa from New Mexico believes the problem is further complicated by the lack of parity between the sexes. In her article, "The Texas T Party " in the April 1990 FIESTA NEWSLETTER, she wrote:

"The first causes of our problems are attitudes of entrenched sexism in this male dominated world. If women weren't regarded as second class citizens, it wouldn't be so bad to want to be like one. The social construction of gender behavior is responsible for many of our more serious problems.

The reason special gender events are important is that we create our own reality, and it works! We are living proof of the right to choose one's own identity, instead of conforming to the status quo white, male dominated system. For me the special gender events are a luxurious bubble bath of communal self-esteem: they make me clean, silky and refreshed. These events stress self-acceptance and the consequent ability to express mutual affection by having fun. By participation in such events we realize that dignity is a reality and we can become dignified as individuals. "

There is an ongoing quest for dignity. Once the individual has reached comfort with self, many transgendered people take the process one step further by attending special events such as the Dignity Cruise. Participants in the cruises have found pride in self-expression, and they have learned to relate personally with love and compassion, not only with other transgendered individuals, but also with the mainstream world.

The main obstacles to personal dignity can be found within the individuals rather than from external stimuli. So what is cross-dressing with dignity? Crossdressing with dignity is a process of moving beyond social stigmas toward self-acceptance. The process begins with honesty with self and is permeated outward to others. The theme is, "To thy own self be true." Step back from the canvas of your life and evaluate your own personal destiny. Unravel the gray bondage of the cocoon that has held you captive. Give yourself permission to be real, dynamic and beautiful in the manner of the butterfly. To paraphrase Emerson:

Though we search the world over for DIGNITY,
We find it within, or we find it not.

GLOSSARY

BULLETIN BOARD SERVICE (BBS). A computer bulletin board service. In 1992 there were over twelve operational transgender computer bulletin board services in this country. In 1999 there are over 12,000 transgender related internet web sites, chat rooms and list services. Transgendered individuals today have the opportunity to obtain information and communicate with other transgendered persons in a non-threatening environment.

CROSSDRESSER. A person, male or female, who wears the clothing of the opposite sex. There are millions of crossdressers in the United States and worldwide.

CROSSDRESSING. The act of wearing the clothing of the opposite sex. It has been estimated there could be as high as ten percent of the total male population who crossdress.

DIGNITY. A self-respecting character or manner. The degree of worth, honor and importance.

DIGNITY CRUISES. A special annual cruise for transgendered persons and their families and friends. On these three to seven day cruises, persons create their own reality, and demonstrate the right to choose an individual identity. The cruises, sponsored by PM Publishers, are the name-sake of this book. For information visit our web site at http://www.pmpub.com or write PM Publishers, P.O. Box 5304, Katy, Texas 77491-5304, or fax 281-347-8747.

EN FEMME. Expressing feminine personality or wearing feminine clothing to express femininity. When en femme, the crossdresser or transgendered individual seeks to project feminine gender behavior.

E .T. V. C. OR EDUCATIONAL TV CHANNEL. A social and educational group representing crossdressers, transgenderists, transsexuals and their partners and friends.

FEMALE IMPERSONATOR. A man who develops his crossdressing into a performing art form. The actors who are female impersonators frequently leave the false impression that all crossdressers are either gay or sexually perverted.

FEMININITY. The doctrine favoring extension of the activities of women in social and political life; the quality of females. The crossdresser wishes to personify his femininity.

FEMMOPHILE. A heterosexual male with a strong love of the feminine. The femmophile has a female component in his personality which is called the femmes self.

GENDER. Masculinity or femininity. Society has assigned a set of traits that are intended to distinguish the gender as either male or female.

GENETIC FEMALE (GF) or GENETIC GIRL (GG). Persons who are born female. A genetic female has an XX chromosome pattern.

GUILT. The fact or state of having done wrong, being guilty, or being to blame. True guilt is related to an obligation one owes oneself. False guilt is felt when a person does not live up to the expectations of others.

HETEROSEXUAL. Characterized by having sexual feelings for persons of the opposite sex. The majority of male crossdressers are said to be heterosexual because they are attracted to women sexually. There are crossdressers who are bisexual or homosexual.

HOMOSEXUAL. Characterized by having sexual feelings for persons of the same sex. The majority of male crossdressers are heterosexual rather than homosexual. A minority of crossdressers may be bisexual with sexual feelings for persons of both sexes.

INTERNATIONAL FOUNDATION FOR GENDER EDUCATION (I. F. G E). An international organization designed to serve as an effective communications, outreach medium, and networking facility for the entire transgendered community and those interested or involved with this community.

MACHO. An especially virile, robust man. The crossdresser attempts to break away from the macho stereotype.

NEGATIVE EMOTIONS. Those emotions associated with the rejection of a natural reality; the emotions associated with questioning the validity of the reality. Transgendered individuals and those who are in relationships with these individuals sometimes feel negative emotions including anger, guilt and fear.

OUTREACH INSTITUTE. An organization which provides effective communications and outreach programs and services for the transgendered community. The Outreach Institute sponsors the annual Fantasia Fair held in Provincetown, Mass. in November.

PASSING. Presenting a credible feminine image to the public.

PERSONALITY BALANCE. A personality characterized by stability, harmony and order. Crossdressers and other trans-gendered individuals with a personality balance have found the perfect blend of masculinity and femininity.

POSITIVE EMOTIONS. Those emotions that move a person in a direction of progress. Thoughtfulness, personal responsibility, love and compassion are examples of positive emotions.

RENAISSANCE. A social and support organization serving the gender community with chapters in several cities and states.

SAFE ENVIRONMENT. An environment that does not force risk-taking. Ideally a crossdresser's home, a transgendered organization meeting or a supportive friend's home would be examples of safe environments for crossdressers.

SECOND SELF. The alternative gender preference of an individual. A person who recognizes and acts upon the presence of both masculine and feminine traits within the personality is said to express a second self. Crossdressers express their second self through feminine clothing and feminine characteristics.

SELF-ACCEPTANCE. The state or quality of being true to oneself. Self-acceptance is frequently the prerequisite for acceptance by others.

SELF-DIGNITY. A feeling of worth, honor, and importance that is not dependent upon the approval of others. Self-dignity is the prerequisite to being perceived by others as dignified.

SELF-IMPRISONMENT. Permitting oneself to be closely confined or restricted. Fear of ridicule or rejection has caused many crossdressers to remain in self-imprisonment.

SEX. Refers to a person's chromosome pattern. A male is a person with an XY sex chromosome pattern; a female has an XX chromosome pattern.

SIGNIFICANT OTHER (S.O.). A wife or a person other than the wife who has a meaningful, important relationship with the crossdresser or transgendered individual. The significant other could be a mother, child, sibling, or close friend, but is not limited to these. An accepting S.O. does much to help the crossdresser.

TRANSGENDERIST (T.G.). A person who makes a permanent change in gender but does not have sexual reassignment surgery. Male crossdressers who are transgenderists live their entire life as women. Female transgenderists live their life as men.

TRANSSEXUAL (TS). A person who has or is planning sexual reassignment surgery. A transsexual actually changes their sex from male to female or from female to male.

TRANSVESTITE (TV). A person who dresses in the clothing of the opposite sex. The word comes from Latin Trans (across) + Vestire (to clothe). Transvestite comedy has made Charlie's Aunt a durable commodity. Crossdressers are transvestites who dress for human fulfillment and not for laughs.

TRI-ESS. The Society for the Second Self. An organization for heterosexual crossdressers and their significant others. Tri-Ess has over forty local chapters in the United States.

APPENDICES

APPENDIX A. / RESEARCH QUESTIONNAIRE

Dear Friend,

Allow me to introduce myself. I am Dr. Peggy Rudd, author of MY HUSBAND WEARS MY CLOTHES. Due to requests from many of you, I have begun research on my next book, CROSS-DRESSING WITH DIGNITY.

I believe that the time is right to move ahead toward the crossdresser's dream of social acceptance. The ultimate goal will be a social situation in which the crossdressing population can lift their heads in dignity. Your participation in this survey could help make this goal a reality.

Please complete the following questionnaire and mail to:

Peggy Rudd

P.O. Box 5304

KATY, TX 77491-5304

(1) How can a crossdresser move beyond the stigmas imposed by society toward crossdressing with dignity?

(2) What obstacles must a crossdresser overcome before he/she reaches this goal?

(3) Fear has been considered a major stumbling block as many crossdressers attempt to gain acceptance. What are your fears and how are you overcoming them?

(4) A guilt-ridden person does not feel dignified. Guilt must be overcome. What things make you feel guilty, and how have you dealt with these issues?

(5) How has crossdressing affected your relationships?

(6) How have you come to self-understanding as related to your crossdressing?

(7) Describe feelings of loneliness that you have experienced. How have you overcome the loneliness?

(8) Have you ever felt a progressive self-improvement as a crossdresser? If so describe the steps utilized to improve your self image and feelings of self-worth.

(9) How did you "break out" of the bondage and become free of the restraints that many crossdressers feel?

(10) What is your formula for being the best person you can be?

(11) What, in your opinion, is involved in crossdressing with dignity?

Please use additional space to write other ideas, special interests or concerns. Please feel free to include anecdotes or stories that could be included in the book. Indicate if you prefer to use your femme name. It is understood that your masculine name will not be used. Your input is vital to the success of this book and is greatly appreciated.

With my gratitude,

Dr. Peggy Rudd

PERSONAL DATA (VOLUNTARY)

Age _____

Marital status _____

Occupation _____

Education _____

Femme name _____

Note: A total of 817 transgendered individuals responded to this survey. It should be noted that respondents listed multiple responses will always exceed 100% of the tables that follow.

APPENDIX B./TABLES

Question One (1) on the questionnaire asks, "How can a crossdresser move beyond the stigmas imposed by society toward crossdressing with dignity?"

Table 5 How Crossdressers Have Moved Beyond Social
   Stigmas

Percent of Respondents Listing Each Item   N=817

ACTIVITY	<30	age range 30-40	41-50	51-60	>60
Develop confidence	03	12	22	35	60
Express the girl within	08	25	40	50	65
Understand God loves me	01	07	08	11	16
Develop a positive attitude	12	23	34	46	65
Stop the denial process	05	25	38	68	89
Reject stereotypes	24	32	43	58	88
Overcome prejudice	06	23	36	57	78
Develop crossdressing culture	35	47	66	80	96
Find safe places to go	25	36	37	66	78
Learn to trust self and others	06	23	33	56	87
Develop compassion	07	28	38	47	79
Overcome negative emotions	30	45	57	70	96
Learn feminine skills	07	24	48	76	90

Table 5 Continued - How Crossdressers Have Moved Beyond Social Stigmas

Percent of Respondents Listing Each Item   N=817

ACTIVITY	age range				
	<30	30-40	41-50	51-60	>60
Decide what you want from life	02	16	36	47	89
Develop good relationships	21	34	50	78	95
Resist provocative behavior	02	14	46	54	66
Educate self and others	22	34	56	88	97
Establish a positive role for women	02	12	33	35	34
Realize there is no cure	03	20	67	86	90
Develop communication skills	04	13	35	45	51
Overcome depression	02	12	23	55	68
Resolve personal concerns	03	14	23	34	54
Be honest with myself	23	31	66	78	89
I have not overcome obstacles	98	53	35	21	01

Note: The last item on this table, "I have not overcome obstacles," was statistically analyzed using the Wilk's lambda. The data have shown this item to be an accurate predictor of the age group of a participant. ($X2=p<.05$)

Question Two (2) on the questionnaire asks, "What obstacles must a crossdresser overcome before he reaches this goal?"

Table 6 What Obstacles Must A Crossdresser Overcome? Percent of Respondents Listing Each Item N=817

OBSTACLE	age range				
	<30	30-40	41-50	51-60	>60
Self-doubt	33	43	41	43	42
Relationship problems	90	91	92	90	89
Moral issues	25	25	30	27	30
Negative self-image	44	43	41	43	41
Denial	78	87	89	86	90
Social stereotypes	67	67	78	88	87
Ridicule/embarrassment	77	67	78	76	55
Prejudice	67	54	56	67	65
Getting older	03	13	34	47	67
Threats to job security	67	88	78	35	02
Lack of trust	12	23	34	43	56
Lack of self-awareness	43	45	66	65	76
Negative emotions	56	78	75	54	76

Table 6 Continued - What Obstacles Must A Crossdresser Overcome?

Percent of Respondents Listing Each Item   N=817

OBSTACLE	age range				
	<30	30-40	41-50	51-60	>60
Negative attitudes	54	65	43	42	56
Feelings of being perverted	67	65	64	66	56
Unfair laws	21	17	12	09	04
Not passing/being read	12	65	51	23	13
Uncertainty about future	23	32	34	25	03
Wanting to be "cured"	65	56	23	11	04
Negative role of women in society	45	21	12	04	05
Physical dangers (attack by a man)	56	34	13	03	01
Depression	34	23	32	32	13
Jealousy of family	54	34	23	12	04
Hate	23	12	05	11	03
Misunderstandings	51	45	22	13	12

Question three (3) asks, "What are your fears and how are you overcoming them?"

Table 7 Dominant Fears As Expressed By Crossdressers

Percent of Respondents Listing This Item   N=817

FEAR	<30	30-40	41-50	51-60	>60
			age range		
Rejection by family	98	70	54	32	12
Loss of employment	90	67	25	13	02
Being discovered	89	78	67	54	11
How crossdressing affects family	90	89	73	62	12
Criticism/ridicule/ verbal abuse	89	78	6	12	02
Being called mentally ill	45	34	21	03	01
Loss of social standing	76	56	45	12	03
Judgment by God	03	11	10	12	02
Being deceptive	54	34	21	12	05
Will I become a transsexual	31	23	16	17	07
Not being attractive	41	43	34	23	12
Growing old	02	01	12	23	24
Being arrested	21	21	23	03	02
Being compulsive/addictive	23	25	17	17	04

Table 8 How Crossdressers Overcome Fears
Percent of Respondents Listing Each Item   N=817

PLAN FOR OVERCOMING FEAR	age range				
	<30	30-40	41-50	51-60	>60
Accept responsibility for feelings	02	12	32	45	56
Make my own decisions	04	15	65	79	89
Educate self and others	05	23	34	54	87
Find someone to talk with	70	74	78	87	89
Avoid high risk situations	05	13	19	45	35
Ask God for help	02	03	11	21	45
Avoid deception	05	12	23	33	04
Take no risks on the job	14	54	46	54	02
Compromise with family members	05	23	34	42	56
Learn to communicate fears	06	15	23	12	23
Develop feminine skills	12	05	24	32	33
Be discrete	05	34	23	19	06
Learn not to let criticisms destroy me	12	16	16	45	56
Make contingency plans	07	06	23	21	12

Table 8 Continued - How Crossdressers Overcome Fears
Percent of Respondents Listing Each Item   N=817

PLAN FOR OVERCOMING FEAR	age range				
	<30	30-40	41-50	51-60	>60
Took responsibility for my actions	03	06	56	67	79
Establish limits on crossdressing	06	07	28	25	12
Never leave the house crossdressed	25	31	05	07	02
Get a post office box to receive correspondence	17	13	23	09	07
Join a support group for crossdressers	17	45	39	74	79
Have female identification card	06	32	21	32	31
Screen catalogs and orders	02	01	02	01	03
Initials of my masculine and feminine names are same	01	02	01	02	02
I have not overcome fear	95	83	64	32	01

Note: The last item on this table,"I have not overcome fear," was statistically analyzed using the Wilk's lambda. The data has shown this item to be an accurate predictor of the age group of research participants with greater than 95% accuracy. (X2=p< .05)

Question four (4) asks, "What things make you feel guilty?"
Table 9 Guilt Feelings Expressed By Crossdressers
Percent of Respondents Listing Each Item   N=817

GUILT	age range				
	<30	30-40	41-50	51-60	>60
No guilt about crossdressing	01	13	35	51	89
Loss of control	54	34	23	12	02
Feminine feelings	87	65	56	12	03
Not sharing total self	65	45	34	12	02
Family deprivation/pain	78	65	56	41	12
Seeing macho in self	07	14	34	13	02
Deception	87	76	56	45	32
Being seen as failure by others due to crossdressing	69	58	31	15	03
Finding too much pleasure in crossdressing	87	76	66	21	03
Returning to male role	35	27	23	12	01
Failure to accept self	80	75	65	34	04
Verbal abuse by others	78	54	42	23	03
Masturbation	93	40	12	07	01
Sexual preference	26	24	16	05	02

Table 9 Continued - Guilt Feelings Expressed By Crossdressers

Percent of Respondents Listing Each Item   N=817

GUILT	<30	age range 30-40	41-50	51-60	>60
Low self-image	90	88	56	21	03
Money spent on crossdressing	54	45	32	12	04
Psychological high related to crossdressing	78	65	56	13	03
Sacrifice of male identity	51	31	24	13	03
Inner reality	78	61	54	17	03
Wearing feminine clothing	79	45	31	11	01
Moral issues	16	23	12	03	01
My personal faults	76	54	43	21	04
Feelings of shame	34	04	12	03	01

Note: The first item on this table, "No guilt about crossdressing," was shown to be an accurate predictor of age group designations of participants. ($X2=p<.05$)

Table 10 How Crossdressers Overcame Guilt

Percent of Respondents Listing Each Item   N=817

METHOD USED TO OVERCOME GUILT	<30	30-40	age range 41-50	51-60	>60
Began to set own standards	02	13	23	32	41
Realized I am hurting no one	03	12	54	60	89
Realized crossdressing is not "bad"	03	16	36	43	92
Looked in the mirror and liked what I saw	14	54	65	67	78
Found others like myself	12	25	37	56	67
Developed self-awareness	11	56	67	78	89
Realized God loves me like I am	01	11	13	16	23
Realized guilt is internal not external	04	21	53	65	76
Realized guilt is a wasted emotion	03	12	24	64	89
Became comfortable with true self	03	13	76	87	98
Realized crossdressing is not pathological	02	15	27	34	67

Question number five (5) asks, "How has crossdressing affected your relationships? "

Table 11 The Effects Of Crossdressing Upon Relationships As Perceived By SINGLE Crossdressers

Items Listed in Rank Order

Most frequent responses

Friends in crossdressing organizations are helpful

No effect at work since no one knows

Non-crossdressing friends have rejected me

Non-crossdressing friends still accept and like me

Engagements were broken because of crossdressing

Because of crossdressing I am more compassionate toward others

It is difficult to find supportive friends

Crossdressing has improved my love making

Because of my crossdressing I show more interest in others

I am not always available to non-crossdressing friends

I have difficulty telling others I am a crossdresser

People don't know about my sexual preference

People are confused about what I am

I tend to reject macho men

Siblings and family members do not accept me

Family members don't want to talk about my crossdressing

Crossdressing helps me relate to others better

Less frequent responses

My knowledge of clothing surprises women

People ask about my shaven legs and arms

Table 12 The Effects Of Crossdressing Upon Relationships As
Perceived By DIVORCED Crossdressers

Items Listed In Rank Order

Most
frequent
responses

Friends in crossdressing organizations are helpful
Crossdressing caused my divorce

Crossdressing was used to alienate my children
against me

Since my divorce, crossdressing has improved
my relationships

Crossdressing has not significantly affected my
relationships

I have become more secretive about my crossdressing
I tend to act macho around others to hide my true self
Crossdressing makes me a better father

Not sharing my crossdressing causes stress

I have difficulty developing secure relationships
because of my crossdressing

I indulge myself

I am reluctant to make a commitment to a relationship
because of my crossdressing

People ask about my shaven legs and arms

Less
frequent
responses

My attempts at purging while married caused extreme
tension

Table 13 The Effects Of Crossdressing Upon Relationships As Perceived By MARRIED Crossdressers

Items Listed In Rank Order

Most frequent responses	People in crossdressing organizations are helpful
	My children have not been affected because of my crossdressing
	My relationships are better because I am a crossdresser
	My wife does not try to accept my crossdressing
	Crossdressing has caused separations from my wife
	My wife tolerates my crossdressing
	Crossdressing causes stress in my family
	My wife worries when I go out crossdressed
	I have told my children, and they are affected by my crossdressing
	My wife does not want me to spend money on crossdressing
	Crossdressing has added dimension to my marriage
	I feel I have cheated my wife because of my crossdressing
	My wife refuses to have sex while I am dressed
	My wife prefers the feminine side of my personality
	My wife does not want me to dress frequently
Less frequent responses	My wife wants me to leave her clothing alone
	Relationships outside the family are not affected since they don't know about my crossdressing

Question six (6) asks, "How have you come to self-understanding as related to your crossdressing?"

Table 14 How Crossdressers Gain Self-Acceptance

Percent of Respondents Listing Each Item   N=817

ACTIVITY	age range				
	<30	30-40	41-50	51-60	>60
Became more feminine	04	06	12	34	43
Set my own standards	03	12	54	87	98
Overcame problems related to crossdressing	04	14	34	49	65
Discovered my value	05	31	67	78	85
Gained courage/confidence	03	08	23	47	89
Developed self-esteem	04	23	43	87	90
Loved myself	03	07	07	56	65
Loved others	12	43	54	50	65
Went to counseling	23	21	14	15	02
Concentrated on my needs	04	21	34	78	89
Grew internally	02	04	06	17	43
Interacted with other crossdressers	13	32	65	76	87
Integrated both genders	02	04	07	14	31

Table 14 Continued - How Crossdressers Gain Self-Acceptance
Percent of Respondents Listing Each Item   N=817

ACTIVITY	age range				
	<30	30-40	41-50	51-60	>60
Helped wife become supportive	03	21	25	32	02
Eliminated negative emotions	02	21	34	87	98
Studied presentation of femininity by others	12	23	32	34	54
Realized crossdressing is not a phase or habit	04	12	67	78	89
Turned to God	01	11	13	12	34
Got rid of macho	04	31	45	56	67
Studied the literature on crossdressing	12	24	32	69	89
Realized my crossdressing is hurting no one	02	04	10	78	89
Realized I am not mentally ill	03	31	56	76	88
I don't accept myself	87	45	31	21	03
Analyzed fetishistic behavior	24	23	21	23	02
Analyzed eroticism related to crossdressing	46	23	11	05	01
Started dressing to fit my age group	05	23	54	66	78

NOTE: The item, "I don't accept myself," was statistically analyzed and found to be an accurate predictor of the age group of participants. ($X2=p<.05$)

Question number seven (7) asks, "Describe feelings of loneliness that you have experienced. How have you overcome the loneliness?"

Table 15 Description of Loneliness As Expressed By Crossdressers

Percent of Respondents Listing Each Item   N=817

	age range				
DESCRIPTOR	<30	30-40	41-50	51-60	>60
Do not feel lonely	02	13	45	67	90
Feel isolated and anxious	56	26	22	12	02
Enjoy being a loner	01	13	14	14	16
Feel trapped by myself	67	56	16	12	03
Feel evil/morally wrong	79	21	11	05	03
Wish I could share my crossdressing with others	87	78	64	66	54
Wish my wife had accepted my crossdressing	24	34	44	35	24
Wish I could talk to someone about my crossdressing	45	26	23	13	03
Feel sexually unfulfilled	56	45	32	23	13
Feel I don't fit in anywhere	43	34	21	12	02
Feel vulnerable to criticism	56	34	31	26	04
Feel I am the only crossdresser in the world	43	34	16	06	01
Feel perverted/a misfit	43	34	23	05	01

Table 15 Continued - Description of Loneliness As Expressed
By Crossdressers

Percent of Respondents Listing Each Item N=817

DESCRIPTOR	age range				
	<30	30-40	41-50	51-60	>60
Feel out of control, compulsive	90	78	51	12	03
Feel mood swings	68	65	32	13	02
Feel deceptive	78	60	45	32	03
Feel depressed and bitter	56	43	32	12	02
Wonder why me?	65	45	31	22	05
Wish God would help me	16	15	06	04	01
Feel rejected	56	34	23	15	02
Feel others believe I am perverted	89	69	54	45	32
Feel utter despair	41	32	21	07	01
Feel alone even in groups	34	25	21	12	01
Wish I could die	03	01	00	00	00
Feel fragile under my mask	34	24	16	11	02
Feel a need to meet other crossdressers	45	45	56	54	34
Feel I must pull away from others to avoid pain	39	31	12	04	03

Table 16 How Crossdressers Have Overcome Loneliness
Percent of Respondents Listing Each Item   N=817

ACTIVITY	<30	30-40	41-50	51-60	>60
Found answers to loneliness within myself	02	13	23	75	97
Corresponded with other crossdressers	41	34	43	43	56
Participated on TV/TS BBS	11	06	12	03	05
Joined an organization for crossdressers	08	34	51	56	67
Attended a crossdressing organization meeting	07	32	50	54	66
Attended a crossdressing organization convention	02	05	16	15	12
Joined a theatre group	05	00	00	00	00
Began a dialogue with self	36	41	45	56	67
Engaged in a rich fantasy life	67	56	34	43	21
Found non-threatening places to go crossdressed	05	04	13	31	14
Came out of the closet	04	12	21	34	56
Got lost in my job and achievements	34	54	56	46	34
Have sex with understanding partner	56	43	34	32	05
Made more friends who understood my crossdressing	34	56	45	65	56
Read crossdressing literature	23	32	45	76	87

age range

Table 16 Continued - How Crossdressers Have Overcome
Loneliness

Percent of Respondents Listing Each Item N=817

ACTIVITY	age range				
	<30	30-40	41-50	51-60	>60
Go shopping while crossdressed	03	04	12	36	45
Go for counseling/therapy	27	19	07	05	03
Dress up at home	36	27	34	31	56
Talked with wife about crossdressing	07	31	31	32	21
Bought a teddy bear	01	00	00	00	00
Gained maturity	04	45	56	78	87
Found contentment in self	03	13	25	53	79
Realized loneliness is a state of mind	07	21	56	65	78
Write, listen to music, etc.	15	12	11	07	09
I have not overcome loneliness	89	74	41	17	02

NOTE: The last item, "I have not overcome loneliness," was found to be an accurate predictor of the age group designations of participants. $(X2=p<.05)$

Question eight (8) asks, "Describe the steps utilized to improve your self-image and feelings of self-worth.

Table 17 Self-Improvement Activities Used By Crossdressers By Specific Age Designation

Age 30 and Younger

Locate open-minded people
Build self-confidence
Improve femininity
Find a good job
Overcome guilt, fear, and
    loneliness
Develop my personality more fully
Improve feminine appearance
Dress for fun and relaxation
Learn how to purchase feminine
    clothing

Age 30-40

Improve feminine
    appearance
Develop feminine personality
Learn more about myself
Try to be the best I can be
Study and read about
    crossdressing
Learn to pass
Join an organization for
    crossdressers
Stop self abuse Learn to survive
Accept myself as I am
Analyze myself/introspection

Age 41-50

Improve my self image
Help others
Accept myself
Observe and learn from others
Join an organization for
    crossdressers
Come out of the closet
Improve emotional status
Become a better human being
Read and study about crossdressing
Improve relationships with others
Get rid of macho Learn to appreciate
    beauty
Improve feelings of self-worth

Age 51-60

Develop feminine personality
Be honest with self and
others about my crossdressing
Improve relationships
Assume more risks
Develop self-esteem
Find God
Reach out and help others
Attend seminars relating to
    crossdressing
Read and study
Learn to blend in when
crossdressed

Table 17 Continued - Self-Improvement Activities Used By Crossdressers By Specific Age Designation

Age 51-60 continued

Get rid of macho
Learn to appreciate beauty
Join organizations for crossdressers

Age 60 and Over

Love myself
Love life
Stop hiding
Join organizations for crossdressers
Find energy-producing activities
Crossdress more frequently
Improve my feminine appearance
Improve my love life
Make the most of each day
Help other people

Question nine (9) asks, "How did you break out of the bondage and become free of the restraints that many crossdressers feel?"

Table 18 Activities Utilized By Crossdressers To Free Feelings of Bondage

Percent of Respondents Listing Each Item   N=817

ACTIVITY	age range				
	<30	30-40	41-50	51-60	>60
No feelings of bondage	02	17	26	34	98
I still feel in bondage	95	45	12	02	00
Revealed my crossdressing to family	05	16	19	34	56
Eliminated negative emotions	05	12	34	89	90
Improved my communication	04	17	45	49	56
Treated myself as a normal person	06	21	67	78	87
Came out of the closet	04	13	34	47	76
Realized my crossdressing is hurting no one	02	34	65	79	93
Got divorced	01	11	16	17	04
Crossdressed more frequently	05	32	66	76	87
Joined an organization for crossdressers	08	29	45	34	65
Participated in gender BBS	17	11	12	04	05

Note: The first two items, "No feelings of bondage," and "I still feel in bondage," were found to be accurate predictors of the age group of participants. ($X2=p<.05$)

Table 18 Continued - Activities Utilized By Crossdressers To Free Feelings Of Bondage

Percent of Respondents Listing Each Item   N=817

ACTIVITY	<30	30-40	41-50	51-60	>60
		age range			
Hit bottom	02	03	04	03	02
Read about crossdressing	56	67	78	65	78
Started sharing my femininity	45	56	76	76	65
Gained confidence and pride	65	57	68	78	87
Took some risks	45	56	65	54	56
Called off the war in me	34	23	43	45	54
Discovered I am not alone	43	34	65	56	76
Asked God for help	02	03	03	04	05
Realized I am getting older	00	01	35	65	78
Stopped thinking of myself as mentally ill	45	24	34	34	43
Stopped deceiving myself and others	04	03	02	02	04
Eliminated the macho in myself	02	03	05	12	45
Dealt with my liabilities	03	01	03	04	05

APPENDIX C./ TRANSGENDER SUPPORT

Tri-Ess (The Society for the Second Self)
8880 Bellaire, B2, Suite 104
Houston, TX 77036
Email: TRIESSINFO@aol.com
Web Site: http://www.tri-ess.org

IFGE (The International Foundation for Gender Education)
Box 229
Waltham, MA 02454-0229
(781) 899-2212
Email: info@ifge.org/
Web Site: http://www.ifge.org/

Renaissance Transgender Association
987 Old Eagle School Rd., Suite 719
Wayne, PA 19087
Email: info@ren.org/
Web Site: http://www.ren.org/

SPICE (Spouses and Partner International Conference for
Education)
PO Box 5304
Katy, TX 77491-5304
Email: desiree1@flash.net
Web Site: http://www.pmpub.com/spice.htm

Dignity Cruises (cruises for transgendered individuals and their
significant others)
PO Box 5304
Katy, TX 77491-5304
Email: melpeg@pmpub.com
Web Site: http://www.pmpub.com/cruise.htm

BIBLIOGRAPHY

Aleta, "Aleta's Coming Out Letter." Denver: GIC Newsletter. 1990.

Allen, C. L., You Are Never Alone. New York: Guidepost Publications. 1979.

Allen, Mariette P., Transformations: Crossdressers and Those Who Love Them, New York: E.P. Dutton, 1998.

Bancroft, J. H., "The Relationship Between Gender Identity and Sexual Behavior: Some Clinical Aspects." In C. Ounsted & D. C. Taylor (Editors.), Gender Differences: Their Ontogeny and Significance. Edinburgh: Churchill Livingstone. 1972.

Bastani, J. B., Kentsmith, D. K., "Psychotherapy With Wives of Sexual Deviants." American Journal of Psychotherapy, 34, 2025.

Benjamin, H., "Transvestism and Transsexualism." American Journal of Psychotherapy. 8, 219-230. 1954.

Bentler, P. M., & Prince, C., "Personality Characteristics of Male Transvestites." III. Journal of Abnormal Psychology. 74, 140-143. 1969

Berendt, John. "High Heel Neil." The New Yorker, January 16, 1995, pp 38-45.

Bornstein, Kate. Gender Outlaw: On Men, Women, and the Rest of Us. New York and London: Routledge, 1994.

Branden, N., How to Raise Your Self Esteem. New York: Bantam Books. 1987.

Brierley, H., Transvestism: Illness, Perversion, or Choice. New York: Pergamon. 1979.

Brown, George R., "Coping With A Transvestite Partner." Medical Aspects of Human Sexuality. 1989.

Bullough, V. L., Bullough, B., and Smith, R. A., "Comparative Study of Male Transvestites, Male to Female Transexuals, and Male Homosexuals." Journal of Sex Research, 19, 238-257. 1983.

Bullough, V. L. & Bullough, Bonnie, <u>Crossdressing, Sex, and Gender.</u> University of Pennsylvania Press, 1993.

Bullough, V.L. & Bullough, Bonnie, "<u>Men Who Crossdress: A Survey</u>."New York: Prometheus Books, 1997.

Casbar, Babs and Carol, "Dignity and Fun on the High Seas: An Account of the Dignity Cruise." <u>Lady-Like Magazine</u> #27, pp 34-36. CDS Publications. 1996.

Coleman, Vernon. Men in Dresses: A Study of Transvestism and Crossdressing. <u>A European Medical Journal Special Report</u>. Bristol, England: J. W. Arrowsmith.1996.

Docter, R. F., <u>Transvestites and Transsexuals, Toward a Theory of Cross-Gender Behavior.</u> London: Plenum Press. 1988.

Elliot, T. S., <u>The Cocktail Party.</u> New York: Harcourt, Brace, and Jovanowich. 1965.

E.T.V.C., "Survey on Family Issues." 1989.

Fairfax, J. E., "How to Tell Your Wife." <u>Tau Chi Handbook.</u> Houston, Texas. Revised Edition 1998.

Fairfax, M. Frances, editor. "Pricilla Queen of the Seas." <u>Femme Mirror</u>. Houston, Texas: Winter 1997.

Feinbloom, D., <u>Transvestites and Transsexuals.</u> New York: Dell. 1976.

Ferguson, Frances. "Pornography: the Theory." <u>Critical Inquiry.</u> 21, pp 670-95. 1995.

Freund, K, Steiner, B. et al. "Two Types of Cross-Gender Identity, <u>Archives of Sexual Behavior,</u> 11, 49-63. 1982.

Jessa, "Texas T Party." Fiesta <u>Chapter Newsletter.</u> 35. 1991.

Jones, B. and L., <u>Men Have Feelings, Too</u>. Book published in 1989 is now out of print.

Hirshfield, M, <u>Die Transvestism</u>. Berlin: Pulvermacher 1987.

Kaplan, M. and D., <u>Smiles.</u> Atlanta: Cheers Publishers. 1984.

Krawetz, M., The Loneliness Remover. New York: Henry Holt. 1989.

Laing, R. D., Self and Others. New York: Pantheon Books. 1969.

Langevin, R., "The Meaning of Cross-dressing." In B. Steiner (Ed.), Gender Dysphoria (pp.207-219). New York: Plenum Press. 1985.

Lanvin, C., "Sensitive New Age Guys." recorded 1989.

Lukianowicz, N., "Survey of Various Aspects of Transvestism in Light of Our Present Knowledge." Journal of Nervous and Mental Disease. 129, 36-64. 1959.

Miller, Rachel. The Bliss of Becoming One. Highland City, Florida: Rainbow Books, Inc., 1996.

Money, J., & Ehrhardt, A. A., Man and Woman, Boy and Girl. Baltimore: Johns Hopkins University Press. 1972.

Offit, Avodahk. The Sexual Self. New York: J. B. Lippincott Co. 1977.

Peo, R. "Crossdressing and the Need For Punishment." Compuserve Gender Line. 1989.

Petterson, K. S. "Fight By the Rules." New York: USA TODAY. 1989.

Pietropinto, A. and Simernauer, J. Beyond the Male Myth, a National Survey. New York: New York Times Books. 1977.

Prince, V. How to Be Woman Though Male. Los Angeles: Chevalier Publications. 1998.

Prince, V. The Crossdresser and His Wife. Los Angeles: Chevalier Publications. Revised Edition, 1998.

Roberts, JoAnn. Coping With Crossdressing. King of Prussia: CDS Publishers. 1995.

Roberts, JoAnn, Coping With Crossdressing Video, King of Prussia, Pa.: CDS Publishers, 1995.

Rowe, Robert J. Bert and Lorie: The Autobiography of a Cross-dresser. Amherst, NY. Prometheus Press, 1997.

Rudd, Peggy J. Crossdressers and Those Who Share Their Lives. Katy, Texas: P.M. Publishers, 1995.

Rudd, Peggy J. My Husband Wears My Clothes. Katy, Texas: P.M. Publishers. Revised edition, 1999.

Rudd, Peggy J. Who's Really From Venus? Katy, Texas: P.M. Publishers, 1998.

Santini, E. A., "On Becoming." Toronto, Canada: Transnews. 1989.

Schott, Richard L. "The Childhood and Family Dynamics of Transvestism." Archives of Sexual Behavior 24, 1995.

Shaw, G. B., Man and Superman. New York: Richard Mansfield, producer. 1903.

Solnit, A., Child Study Center, Yale University, A Published Study. Associated Press International. 1989.

Stern, K. The Flight From Woman. New York: Farrar, Staus, and Giroux. 1965.

Tanksley, P. Love Gift. Old Tappan, New Jersey: Fleming H. Revell Company. 1971.

Thorne, M., "LSD and Marital Therapy With a Transvestite and His Wife." Journal of Sex Research. 1967.

Thorne, Peggy R. Love Calendar, The Secrets of Love. Katy, Texas. P.M. Publishers. 1993.

Walker, A. Horses Make the Landscape More Beautiful. New York: Harcourt, Brace, Jovanovich. 1984.

Wise, T. N. "Coping With a Transvestite Mate.: Clinical Implications. "Journal of Sex and Marital Therapy. 11: 293-300.

Wise, T. N., Meyer, J. K., "The Border Area Between Transvestism and Gender Dysphoria: Transvestite Applicants for Sex Reassignment." Archives of Sexual Behavior. 9, 327-342. 1980.

INDEX

ORDER FORM MAY BE DUPLICATED

———— **My Husband Wears My Clothes** $14.95

———— **Who's Really From Venus?** $15.95

———— **Crossdressers: And Those Who Share Their Lives** $14.95

———— **Crossdressing With Dignity** $14.95

———— **Love Calendar: The Secrets of Love** $9.95 reduced to $4.95

———— Sub-total

———— 10% Discount or 20% discount 3 or more books

———— Sales tax - Texas residents add 08%

———— Shipping 10% of total order domestic or 15% of total order for international. For air mail international add $2.00 each book

———— Total

You may pay by check, money order or credit card:

Credit Cards: ( ) Visa ( ) Mastercard ( ) Discover ( ) AX

_____ _____
   Credit Card Number   Exp. Date

_____
       Name On Card

_____
Street   City   State   Zip Code

_____
      Signature   Email

Mail or fax to:

PM Publishers
P.O. Box 5304
Katy, TX 77491-5304
Fax: (281) 347-8747
Email: pmpub@pmpub.com
Secure ordering at: http://www.pmpub.com/books.htm